We Preach Christ Crucified

SERMONS OF GERHARD O. FORDE

Marianna Forde, Editor

Lutheran University Press
Minneapolis, Minnesota

We Preach Christ Crucified
SERMONS OF GERHARD O. FORDE
Marianna Forde, Editor

Copyright © 2016 Marianna L. Forde Trust. All rights reserved. Published by Lutheran University Press, an imprint of 1517 Media. No part of this book may be reproduced or transmitted in any form by any means, electronic, mechanical, recording, or otherwise, without the express permission of the publisher. For information or permission for reprints or excerpts, please contact the publisher.

Some scripture quotations are from the Revised Standard Version of the Bible, copyright © 1946, 1952, and 1971 National Council of the Churches of Christ in the United States of America. Used by permission. All rights reserved worldwide. Other scripture quotations are from the New Revised Standard Version Bible, copyright © 1989 National Council of the Churches of Christ in the United States of America. Used by permission. All rights reserved worldwide.

ISBN-13: 978-1-942304-24-1
eISBN: 978-1-942304-99-9

Contents

Preface			5
1	Without a Card	Psalm 19	7
2	Food and Drink Indeed!	John 6:53-60	10
3	The Lord's Supper	1 Corinthians 11:23-26	12
4	The Kingdom of Heaven	Matthew 22:1-14	17
5	A Voice Says, "Cry!"	Isaiah 40:6-11	20
6	He Who Comes	Luke 3:1-14	23
7	He Who Is to Come	Matthew 11:2-11	27
8	And Lo, the Star	Matthew 2:9-11	31
9	Healing	Matthew 8:1-13	34
10	On the God-ness of God	John 1:43-51	40
11	Whoever Would Save His Life	Luke 9:24	44
12	Sin and Grace	Romans 6:1-11	47
13	For to Me to Live Is Christ	Philippians 1:21	51
14	For God So Loved the World	John 3:16-17	54
15	Give Thanks to the Lord	Psalm 106:1	57
16	Loose Ends?	Psalm 65:5	60
17	Good and Evil	Luke 11:24-26	63
18	On Sin	Genesis 2:15-17; 3:1-13	65
19	My God, My God, Why Have You Forsaken Me?	Matthew 27:46	72
20	Father, Forgive Them	Luke 23:34	76
21	Testimony	1 Corinthians 2:1-2; 2 Corinthians 4:5-6	78
22	Forgetting and Remembering	Psalm 13	81
23	Faith and Doubt	John 20:19-29	84
24	Something for Nothing	Matthew 9:2-7	89
Endnotes			92

Gerhard O. Forde

Preface

Renowned Lutheran theologian Gerhard O. Forde was a professor at Luther Seminary in St. Paul, Minnesota, for thirty-four years. He participated in international Luther Congresses, acting as president when the Congress met in Minnesota in 1993. He was also a member of the national Lutheran-Roman Catholic Dialogues in the United States for over twenty years.

Gerhard is remembered by his former students and by the church for his strong commitment to proclamation. His book, *Theology Is For Proclamation*, develops his thinking on this subject. He makes clear the importance of this mission in a statement in his Introduction: "Proclamation, as we shall use the term in this study, is explicit declaration of the good news, the gospel, the *kerygma*."[1] His seminary classes were notable for his frequent shifting from secondary to primary discourse to proclaim the gospel as clearly as possible to his students, beginning in the classroom.

A number of Gerhard's sermons have been published elsewhere. This present collection offers twenty-four previously unpublished sermons, some preached at churches, more at Luther Seminary chapel. Where not specifically designated for the chapel by Gerhard on the sermon manuscript, others imply that audience by their context. All testify to Gerhard's concern for preaching the gospel, sprinkled here and there with his well-known sense of humor.

It should be noted here that Gerhard's language was maintained. So, for example, pronouns are often masculine, although they are meant to be inclusive. Such language use reflects the time the sermons were written.

Without a Card

What is creation? Creation, someone has aptly said, is like a big bouquet of flowers—with no card. If a messenger were to come to your door one fine day and present you with such a bouquet—with no card—what would you do? Like all the sons and daughters of Adam, I expect you would be puzzled. Your most immediate reaction would probably be that there must be some mistake and you would ask the messenger whether he hadn't got the wrong address and shouldn't take it back. But if the messenger is adamant and insists that it was indeed meant for you, what would be your next move? It would be, I expect, that you would begin to feel a bit uneasy. You would begin to wonder: "What does it mean?" "What does the sender of the bouquet intend?" Given the nature of the times, you might even rummage through the bouquet to make sure there were no booby traps! Being satisfied that there weren't, you might begin to look more closely at the bouquet itself. "Is there some secret message here?" "What is the hidden agenda behind the bouquet?" "Is there some secret language waiting to be decoded?" Perhaps there are some roses there. What does that mean? Love? Or maybe there are some chrysanthemums. Does that mean death? (Some people think so!) Or perhaps there are even some thistles and thorns that prevent you from getting too cozy with your bouquet.

At any rate, you would probably bend every effort trying to decipher what stands behind the bouquet, to find the secret of what it means for you and your life. Is the giver some secret admirer of mine? Or is the giver setting me up for something? Or is the giver trying to buy me? What's it all about anyway?

And while you are thus musing with yourself and trying to grasp the meaning of it all, you would probably begin to notice something even more reprehensible about your bouquet: it's dying. Just imagine that! It's dying—even before you have had a chance to figure out what it is all about, to find the key to this moment in your life. Now you may, and perhaps would, at this point, take some steps to keep it alive. You might even, in your frustration or fatigue at efforts to keep it alive, seek to replace your bouquet with a set of plastic flowers. But that is perhaps the ultimate blasphemy! Who wants plastic flowers? They don't tell us anything; they only deceive. Besides, they can't even die, so who needs to pay any attention to them at all? And so one arrives at last, at a kind of living death, an ersatz eternity.

So what does it all add up to? There is no card; there is just the bouquet given to us. It lives for a time, and it dies. But perhaps in the midst of it all, in the muddle of our concern to find the secret, to wring some meaning from it, to use it for our own selfish ends—perhaps in the midst of all that we simply miss the obvious. It is just a gift! There is no hidden agenda. It is simply itself; it told its own story. As the psalmist put it:

> The heavens are telling the glory of God:
> And the firmament proclaims his handiwork.
> Day to day pours forth speech
> And night to night declares knowledge.

And yet:

> There is no speech, nor are there words;
> Their voice is not heard;
> Yet their voice goes out through all the earth,
> And their words to the end of the world.

It seems somehow awfully hard for us to learn that lesson: that there is no hidden agenda. God gives his rain to fall on the just and on the unjust. Or as Luther put it in the explanation to the fourth petition of the Lord's Prayer:

> Give us this day our daily bread: What does this mean? God indeed gives daily bread without our prayer, even to all the wicked. But we pray in this petition that he would teach us to acknowledge it as his gift and receive it with thanksgiving and praise.

There's the rub! We have a hard time with that. We have a hard time seeing that it is all right there before our eyes, asking simply that we pay attention and care. For our days too, we are reminded, are as grass, and as the flower of the field that withers and dies—and we have no plastic substitutes. It is hard for us to learn the lesson of creation. We listen rather to the voice of the tempter: "You shall not die, you shall be as gods." We seek the secret behind the scenes, to wrest from creation the answer to our agony, to go on living as long as possible at any cost, and perhaps even, if we can manage it, grasp at some sort of plastic immortality. Even much of the current concern about ecology—justified as that is—is fired, I fear, by our same old lust and greed to live at all costs. We are learning, perhaps, that we can't get away with as much as we thought we could.

It is hard to learn the lesson of creation, to grasp that there is no hidden agenda, that there is just the gift to be enjoyed and cared for. That is why, I suspect, we shall have to learn the lesson truly only from the One who came to us with no hidden agenda—the One who simply gave himself for us to the death in order that we might live; that we might be made new creatures and learn to live for our time and love and care—and pay attention! It was in him, we are told, that all things were created, and all things will be consummated. He is, so to speak, the card on the bouquet, and he brings home the final truth: It is all a gift! He gave it and he will carry it to completion. So it is just a gift for you! Rejoice! Be glad! And take care!

Sermon preached at Luther Seminary chapel, February 1975

Food and Drink Indeed!

> *Jesus said to them, "Truly, truly, I say to you, unless you eat the flesh of the Son of man and drink his blood, you have no life in you; he who eats my flesh and drinks my blood has eternal life, and I will raise him up at the last day. For my flesh is food indeed, and my blood is drink indeed. He who eats my flesh and drinks my blood abides in me, and I in him. As the living Father sent me, and I live because of the Father, so he who eats me will live because of me. This is the bread which came down from heaven, not such as the fathers ate and died; he who eats this bread will live forever." This he said in the synagogue, as he taught at Capernaum. Many of his disciples, when they heard it, said, "This is a hard saying; who can listen to it?"*
>
> JOHN 6:53-60 RSV

"My flesh is food indeed, and my blood is drink indeed." For some time now it has seemed ironic to me that we should march daily into this place under the auspices of a sign which boldly announces, "NO FOOD OR BEVERAGE IN THE CHAPEL!" Now, I hope that is just a prohibition, not a prediction! Sanna will bear witness that I have protested that the sign ought to be taken down, at least on Wednesdays! In any case, I am here to announce that today, at least, according to the promise in our text, there is indeed food and drink in the chapel, and that it is for you.

And this is not, of course, a laughing matter, because your eternal salvation hangs in the balance. As our text warns us, all is not sweetness and light; there is danger here. "This is a hard saying, who can listen to it?" It is, in the first instance, no doubt offensive that there should be this sign, something so mundane as food and beverage in the chapel. We come, I expect, thinking to find something much more spiritual, more exalted, some splendid thought, some wonderful and enlightening idea, something that really meets our needs and makes us feel good. But what we find is a piece of bread and a sip of wine blocking our way. Regin Prenter put it this way:

> External signs—in all their poverty and insignificance, in their concrete appearance as an unimportant straw—obstruct all ways of our own to God, and they only leave open God's own concrete, unforeseen, incalculable, and inexplicable way. Where we depart from these outward signs, such as baptism, preaching, the Lord's Supper, it always means that we are beginning to enter the dangerous way of speculation or work toward *Deus nudus*.[2]

Yes, the shock of just food and drink blocks our ways to God. But that, of course, is a good thing—that is just as it should be—because at the same time it opens up the possibility of God's way to us. For if, perchance, you are poor in spirit, if, like me, you have a hard time with heavy spiritual talk, if you don't know what in the world it means to have Jesus in your heart or just exactly what or how it is you are supposed to feel about it all, then come, eat and drink. Let it roll around on your tongue. Taste it. And know that is all, really, you have to feel. It is a foretaste of the way it's going to be in the end. "This is the bread which came down from heaven, not such as the fathers ate and died; whoever eats this bread will live forever."

Yes, friend, there is food and drink in the chapel, and it is for you.

Sermon preached at Luther Seminary chapel, April 28, 1993

The Lord's Supper

My purpose in coming to you as I understand it is to talk and discuss with you some of the basic features of our Lutheran understanding of the faith. Since this is a day on which you are partaking of the Lord's Supper, I thought it perhaps would be appropriate in this sermon to say something about what Lutherans have taught and believed about the supper of our Lord. The text which stands behind my words is taken from the eleventh chapter of St. Paul's first letter to the Corinthians, beginning at the twenty-third verse:

> For I received from the Lord what I also delivered to you, that the Lord Jesus on the night when he was betrayed took bread, and when he had given thanks, he broke it, and said, "This is my body which is for you. Do this in remembrance of me." In the same way also the cup, after supper, saying, "This cup is the new covenant in my blood. Do this, as often as you drink it, in remembrance of me." For as often as you eat this bread and drink the cup, you proclaim the Lord's death until he comes (1 Corinthians 11:23-26 RSV).

What have we Lutherans understood by these words? As you are no doubt aware, Luther and the Lutheran church which followed him have always insisted that the words mean just exactly what they say, according to the word and promise of our Lord. This bread which we eat *is* the body of our Lord, this cup *is* his blood, and it is given *to you* in the action of the sacrament. Lutherans, that is to say, have always insisted on the *real presence* of the body and blood of the crucified and risen Lord in the Supper. It is *his* supper, *his* way of coming to us. He has decided to meet us here, in this place, at this time, in, with and under this bit of bread and this cup of wine.

It always has been somewhat difficult, I suppose, for us to grasp why Luther and the Lutheran tradition have been so insistent on this. So it is perhaps well for us once in a while to deal with the question and to refresh our memories about it. The first and most important, and the most simple, answer to why Lutherans have been so insistent on the presence of the body and blood of our Lord in, with, and under the bread and the wine is that that is what the Word, the promise, of God says. It is Good News. God's word means what it says, and God does not lie. God promises to be here for you, and God will never, *never,* go back on his promises. If he says it, he will do it. You can count on that. To believe God is simply to take him at his word. When God says, "Here I am for you," then, as Luther puts it, you can say, "Here I have him. . . . I can count on that, forever." We have never attempted to explain or figure out *how* he could be present in bread and wine. If we can say it without seeming too irreverent we can simply say, "That is his problem!" He has promised to do it, and he will do it. He, after all, is the almighty creator of heaven and earth, and it should pose no particular difficulty for him!

But even though we have made no consistent efforts to explain *how* God could be present here, it is important, I think, to try to grasp *why* this insistence on the real presence of our Lord is so crucial for the understanding of the Christian faith. When we ask this question, we get into the basic nature of what faith is all about. Faith, you see, has to do with God, with that very God who is the almighty creator of heaven and earth. Faith has to do with God and his decisions, not merely with us and what we may or may not have decided. There is something about us—I suppose it is our particular kind of self-centeredness and perversity—that makes us always want to talk and think about ourselves, our doings, our decisions, our piety, our religiousness. But that is not what faith has to do with in the first instance. It has to do with God. For God has made a decision about you. He has decided, in his mercy, in his lovingkindness, in his almightiness, what to do about you. Now, no doubt that scares us a bit; it may even make us a bit—perhaps even more than a bit—angry. We like to control our own destiny; we tell ourselves we would like to control the ultimate outcome of things. But when you think about it, that is really quite a blasphemous claim on our part. What we are really saying, and perhaps what we are really thinking in our heart of hearts, is that we think it would be better if we decided what is to happen to us, that things would turn out better that way, that it would perhaps be safer—safer if we were to decide who are to be the eventual citizens of God's eternal Kingdom. Can we really say that? With any degree of confidence? Would that not really be a mark of supreme distrust of God to say that? What we would really be saying is something like this: God, I can't trust you with the outcome of the world, the outcome of my life, or anyone's life. Therefore, I think it would be better if I decided how things are to turn out! Certainly that would be blasphemy, would it not? Blasphemy of the highest order! That is, as a matter of fact, the very thing that the Christian tradition has called original sin—the sin of mistrust, disbelief in God, the attempt to take things into our own hands, to listen to the temptation of the serpent: You shall be as God!

So the Christian faith has to do with God. It has to do with what God has decided. For he *is* God, and there is nothing any of us can do about that!

Now since that is the case, since God has made a decision about you, and if you are worried about that, then the only thing to do is to pay attention, to look and see *what* it is that he has decided. We get worried when we think or hear about God's decision because we begin to think that perhaps he has decided something off in eternity about us without really letting us in on it. But now the *whole point* of it all is that that is just exactly *not* what he has decided to do. He has decided to *reveal* right down here on earth what it is he wants to do about you. He has decided to send Jesus, his Son, to cure you of all your fears, all your mistrust. He has decided not to push you around; he has decided to save you. He has decided, in short, to make a new being of you. He has decided to send his witnesses to you, his ministers to you, and has given them the authority, the unheard-of authority to say in his behalf, "You are mine, and I will not let you go." He has decided to be for you—all the way to death and beyond.

That is what the Lord's Supper, finally, is all about. He has decided to meet you here, at this time, at this place, to say: Here is my body and blood. It is for you; you are mine! Is that not fantastic? The whole question of what God may or may not have decided in eternity is answered here. It is answered in your baptism; it is answered in the preaching of the gospel, in the pronouncement of the forgiveness of sins which we have just heard; it is answered in the sacrament where we have communion with him and with all his saints. He has decided to meet you here, to be for you, all the way. Here, you can say, as Luther said, I have him. That is why, Luther insisted, his presence here is *real*. He has decided to be here for you, and he does not lie. You can count on him.

Perhaps if we see this, we can begin to get a glimpse somewhat at least, of why it is that he has decided to be here for you in just this particular way, in this bit of bread and this cup of wine. Luther, in his characteristic bluntness, says in one instance that God chose these lowly means, this bread and wine, so that "clever arrogant spirits and reason be blinded and disgraced in order that the proud may stumble and fall and never partake of Christ's supper; and on the other hand that the humble may be warned and may arise...and partake...." What did he mean by that? He meant, I suppose, that we are by nature rather arrogant when it comes to things religious. We either think we are very pious or at least that we ought to be. It seems somehow incredible to us that God should have stooped to such lowly means as this. We would like to think, perhaps, that what goes on here is only symbolic of something much more spiritual which goes on somewhere else—perhaps within our minds or in heaven or somewhere else. We are, you might say, much too religious for God. That is why we think most of the time we can get along without him. *But God, of course, has a motive in all of this.* He is not interested in the religious beings we think we are; that of course, is just what Jesus' arguments with the Pharisees were all about. God is out to remake us, to make us new beings, to regenerate us, to cause us to be reborn— reborn as the creatures of this earth he intended us to be when he created Adam. We fly too high and mighty, one way or another. In both our religion and our irreligion, we think we don't need God. So he takes a bit of bread and a cup of wine and says, "Here, this is my body, this is my blood, come back to earth, to the good earth God has created and be reborn for this earth, reborn for the earth that God intended; and have no fear, he who eats this bread and drinks this cup will live—forever."

And perhaps, just perhaps, we can begin to get a glimpse of what God is up to in all of this, why he takes the bread and the wine as the means through which to get through to us once again. In our fallen world, bread and wine, food and drink is what we seek. We work, we grasp and hoard, scrimp and save. We fight over it, and oppress people for it, seek to gain every advantage to get it. It divides us into classes, rich and poor, upper, lower, and middle, Black and white. But here God says, "This bread, this wine, this is my body, my blood." This is mine, and I mean to have it back. And it is free, absolutely free. There are no differences at my table. All are one here. Here you come, rich and poor, high and low; here you come with that person on the other end of the pew, perhaps, whose politics you can't stand, or whom you don't like or can't abide. For here you have to do with what God has decided to do about us. It is a sign, a sign of that great eschatological banquet, that final banquet in which God's will finally will be done. It is the promise that this is the way it is going to be one day, by the grace of God. For God has decided to do a new thing, to make all things new—even to make you new.

So, my friend, if you haven't heard it before, hear it now. God has decided to do something about you. And here it all is! Come, eat, drink, believe, and be glad. It is for real. He has decided to save you.

The Kingdom of Heaven

> *And again Jesus spoke to them in parables, saying, "The kingdom of heaven may be compared to a king who gave a marriage feast for his son, and sent his servants to call those who were invited to the marriage feast; but they would not come. Again he sent other servants, saying, 'Tell those who are invited, Behold, I have made ready my dinner, my oxen and my fat calves are killed, and everything is ready; come to the marriage feast.' But they made light of it and went off, one to his farm, another to his business, while the rest seized his servants, treated them shamefully, and killed them. The king was angry, and he sent his troops and destroyed those murderers and burned their city. Then he said to his servants, 'The wedding is ready, but those invited were not worthy. Go therefore to the thoroughfares, and invite to the marriage feast as many as you find.' And those servants went out into the streets and gathered all whom they found, both bad and good; so the wedding hall was filled with guests.*
>
> *"But when the king came in to look at the guests, he saw there a man who had no wedding garment; and he said to him, 'Friend, how did you get in here without a wedding garment?' And he was speechless. Then the king said to the attendants, 'Bind him hand and foot, and cast him into the outer darkness; there men will weep and gnash their teeth.' For many are called, but few are chosen."*
>
> MATTHEW 22:1-14 RSV

Our text today compares the Kingdom of heaven to a wedding feast to which the king sends out a great and urgent invitation. The invitation, we are told, was rather badly received by those invited. The bearers of the invitation are maltreated and killed, and those originally invited subsequently punished by the king. Then the king sends his emissaries out into the thoroughfares to gather in everyone they can, good and bad, so that the king will have his celebration nevertheless and the wedding hall be filled with guests.

All of this is relatively straightforward, and we feel that in the context of Jesus' ministry we can grasp pretty well what it means. But the incident which really brings us up short is that of the unfortunate fellow who had gotten in without a wedding garment. He was summarily bound hand and foot and cast into the outer darkness where there is weeping and gnashing of teeth. Now in places where the general attitude might be that sloppiness is next to godliness, it might seem that that is rather harsh treatment for one whose only offense seems to be that he was improperly dressed!

What really was wrong? It would be tempting—and perhaps not entirely out of place at this point—to launch into a discourse on the virtues of proper dress, both liturgically and otherwise. But for the moment, at least, I won't succumb to that temptation. There have been many attempts, I suppose, in the history of interpretation to explain, perhaps even explain *away* or allegorize away the embarrassment which the text occasions. I have heard many sermons in which the general idea was that the wedding garment was really the imputed righteousness of Christ, and that what the man lacked was justification by faith or something like that. Perhaps there is a sense in which such interpretation is not so bad, but really it is, I think, an unnecessary kind of allegorization. For I wonder if the answer is not much more simple. The point is that the invitation is to a feast, and a feast calls for celebration, and a celebration calls for a festive and joyous response to the invitation. It didn't, in the final analysis, make any difference if those who responded were rich or poor, good or bad, great or little; the one thing that was important was that they come prepared to celebrate. The man who came without a wedding garment was one, no doubt, who didn't really grasp what was going on. He came, no doubt, under some sort of compulsion or sense of duty. He reasoned, perhaps, that since the king commanded, he had jolly well better put in an appearance, and the little matter of the wedding garment didn't matter as long as he showed up, however grudgingly. He came not because he really wanted to, but because he was more afraid of what might happen if he didn't.

So he showed up, but in his work pants! But then comes the agonizing moment of reckoning. The king spies him suddenly and asks, "What are you doing here? This is a celebration!" He was speechless.

When God calls us into his Kingdom he calls us to celebrate! That is the point! And those who come unprepared to celebrate, those who come because they think they ought to or they are really more afraid of what might happen if they don't come, those who come out of a dull and gloomy sense of duty—those who come in that way decline and spurn the invitation just as surely as those who are unwilling to come at all. For the Kingdom of heaven is like a great feast! Everything is prepared; everything is ready! And the only response to such an invitation can be to celebrate! To enter into it whole-heartedly and with joy. That is what we are called upon to do when we come here to worship: to celebrate! That is what we are called upon to do when we take up the task of theology. For theology, as Karl Barth has put it, is a happy science.

For the Kingdom of God is like a great feast! So above all, come prepared to celebrate!

Sermon preached at Luther Seminary chapel, September 26, 1966

A Voice Says, "Cry!"

A voice says, "Cry!" and I said, "What shall I cry?" All flesh is grass, and all its beauty is like the flower of the field. The grass withers, the flower fades, when the breath of the Lord blows upon it; surely the people is grass. The grass withers, the flower fades; but the word of our God will stand forever. Get you up to a high mountain, O Zion, herald of good tidings; lift up your voice with strength, O Jerusalem, herald of good tidings, lift it up, fear not; say to the cities of Judah, "Behold your God!" Behold, the Lord God comes with might, and his arm rules for him; behold, his reward is with him, and his recompense before him. He will feed his flock like a shepherd, he will gather the lambs in his arms, he will carry them in his bosom, and gently lead those that are with young.

ISAIAH 40:6-11 RSV

Is someone coming? Will anyone come? This is a question which is asked in many ways and for many different reasons among us mortals. It is asked in fear and trembling by the mischievous child or by those outside the law, the thief or the murderer. It is asked in fright by those who have gone astray in strange and hostile places. It is asked in hope by the shipwrecked thrown suddenly out of the way and out of touch on the seas or by those lost in the wilderness. It is asked in longing by the old, forgotten by their children and their loved ones, or by the lonely, searching for a glance of recognition in the empty faces of the crowd.

Is someone coming? Will anyone come? In a deeper sense, in the sense of what we like to call the spiritual, it is a question which we all ask one way or another—perhaps partly in fear, partly in hope, partly in longing. For it is a question about the meaning of life. In this deeper sense all of us are outside the law, all of us have gone astray in a strange and hostile place; we are shipwrecked, out of the way, out of touch, lost, forgotten, lonely. And the ultimate question for us is: Is someone coming? Will anyone come? Is there anyone there—outside, beyond, in the depths, anywhere—who will come and find us, or are we after all alone in a world which is growing cold?

And this is the question which is asked by the prophet in our text. He writes: "A voice says, 'Cry!' and I said, 'What shall I cry?' All flesh is grass and all its beauty is like the flower of the field. The grass withers, the flower fades, when the breath of the Lord blows upon it; surely the people is grass." There is nothing here to shout about, the prophet says, nothing to say, nothing to tell the people. All the beauty, all the greatness of our achievements, though they may impress us momentarily will have an end. Is there someone coming? As far as eye can see, there is no answer.

We are entering now the Advent season. And the message of the Advent season is the tremendous claim that someone is coming—someone who has come, someone who is coming, and someone who will come again. That which no eye has seen, or no ear has heard, what could not have entered into the heart of man—that is happening. Someone is coming! To be sure the grass withers, the flower fades, *but*—and that is the important thing—the word of our God will stand forever. There is after all something to say; we have something to tell one another. God has promised, and his word shall stand. Therefore the prophet goes on to declare: "Get you up to a high mountain, O Zion, herald of good tidings; lift up your voice with strength, O Jerusalem, herald of good tidings; lift it up, fear not; say to the cities of Judah, 'Behold your God!' Behold, the Lord God comes with might, and his arm rules for him. . . . He will feed his flock like a shepherd, he will gather the lambs in his arms, he will carry them in his bosom, and gently lead those who are with young."

Someone is coming. This is the message of Advent. The prophet who cried these words was sure that someone would come. And we now in this season celebrate him who has come. To be sure, the way he takes may seem strange to us, and we could wish perhaps that he would have taken some other way or made it more obvious. He was born in an out-of-the-way place, he rides into Jerusalem on an ass, and he leaves by way of being executed as a common criminal. He comes and goes in such a way that most people don't even know he has been here. We don't know, ultimately I guess, just why he took this way—but it is his way. Perhaps he did it this way because he knows that we are really a hard lot to reach. In spite of our longing we are also half rebellious and afraid. We all have our own thinking about the way in which he should have come. We want someone to come, but we are also afraid of what that might mean. As Frances Thompson put it: "I was sore adread lest having thee, I might have nought beside." So he comes in his own way—to see if perhaps he can find his way into our hearts. For really, that is the only kind of coming that matters. Kings we have had plenty of. Dictators we can do without. Moral reformers we get tired of pretty fast. Philosophers come and go like women's fashions. But he comes quietly, in meekness and lowliness, in his own way. He does not force himself upon us, he does not shove anyone around—he comes and goes in his own way—the way of the cross. He knows that the only coming which can be of any real importance to us is the one which will change our hearts, quiet our fears, and set us free. This is his way.

Someone is coming. It is a daring proclamation. Among the words of men there is none more unexpected, more audacious than this. But the prophet says, "Lift up your voice with strength . . . lift it up, fear not; say to the cities of Judah, 'Behold your God!' Behold, the Lord God comes with might." He is coming. Will he find you? How will you receive him? That is something only you can answer. The message of Advent is this: Prepare the way, repent, and believe.

He Who Comes

In the fifteenth year of the reign of Tiberi-us Caesar, Ponti-us Pilate being governor of Judea, and Herod being tetrarch of Galilee, and his brother Philip tetrarch of the region of Ituraea and Trachonitis, and Lysani-as tetrarch of Abilene, in the high-priesthood of Annas and Caiaphas, the word of God came to John the son of Zechariah in the wilderness; and he went into all the region about the Jordan, preaching a baptism of repentance for the forgiveness of sins. As it is written in the book of the words of Isaiah the prophet,

> *"The voice of one crying in the wilderness:*
> *Prepare the way of the Lord,*
> *make his paths straight.*
> *Every valley shall be filled,*
> *and every mountain and hill shall be brought low,*
> *and the crooked shall be made straight,*
> *and the rough ways shall be made smooth;*
> *and all flesh shall see the salvation of God."*

He said therefore to the multitudes that came out to be baptized by him, "You brood of vipers! Who warned you to flee from the wrath to come? Bear fruits that befit repentance, and do not begin to say to yourselves, 'We have Abraham as our father'; for I tell you, God is able from these stones to raise up children to Abraham. Even now the axe is laid to the root of the trees; every tree therefore that does not bear good fruit is cut down and thrown into the fire."

And the multitudes asked him, "What then shall we do?" And he answered them, "He who has two coats, let him share with him who has none; and he who has food, let him do

> *likewise."* Tax collectors also came to be baptized, and said to him, "Teacher, what shall we do?" And he said to them, "Collect no more than is appointed you." Soldiers also asked him, "And we, what shall we do?" And he said to them, "Rob no one by violence or by false accusation, and be content with your wages."
>
> LUKE 3:1-14 RSV

Our text is an Advent text, the announcement of the coming of the Lord by John the Baptist. The announcement, it seems, threw people into considerable consternation—so much so that they were led to cry out, "What then shall we do?" And John's answer is direct and unequivocal: "Bear fruits that befit repentance . . . He who has two coats, let him share with him who has none; and he who has food, let him do likewise. . . . Even now the axe is laid to the root of the trees; every tree therefore that does not bear good fruit is cut down and thrown into the fire." That's the way it is when the Lord comes.

In our day, when some seem to be alarmed about the apparent rebirth of that nasty thing called "the social gospel" and like movements, I suppose there might be some nervousness about the manner in which John the Baptist moves so immediately from the coming of the Lord to giving away your coat and sharing your food. We would much rather, I suppose, that he had spent much more time in transition, explaining how the coming of the Lord means first of all that we should devote ourselves to the cultivation of our piety, or pointing out that the gospel really has to do only with man's relationship to God and getting all that business straight and that anything else is really not the business of the preacher, or at least strictly secondary if one really ought to get around to it at all. We would like, I expect, if we could make more of a gap between the coming of the Lord and giving away our extra coat—a gap which we could fill with a lot of theological padding and insulation and junk and garbage so that movement from one to the other isn't really so painfully immediate and sequential. It may be true that much needs to be said about the bad theology of the social gospel movement, but it is also true that we too must realize that it is terribly easy to set up our theology as a buffer against the real coming of the Lord and its consequences. Indeed, one wonders if today we have not become past masters at it. And perhaps it is precisely that sort of thing which John is preaching against.

For what does it mean to say that the Lord is coming? Indeed, that he *has* and *will* come? It means that the Lord whom we worship and proclaim in the Christian church is one who comes to us in such a way that we do not need to go to him. Indeed, it must be put even more sharply. It is not merely that we do not *need* to go to him, it is rather that we *cannot* go to him; it is no longer even an option. He is the one who comes to you, in his own way; there is nothing you can do about it. He completely reverses the direction of what usually goes by the name of religion. He comes to you so that there is absolutely nothing you can do but repent and then live like you believed it—bear fruit that benefits repentance. No other option is open.

I wonder sometimes if we really get the point of all this. If the real bite of it comes home to us. Even our usual manner of speaking, theologically, it seems to me, militates against a proper understanding. We talk about ourselves as "fallen creatures." And by that we give the impression that our trouble is that we started out somewhere higher up on the way to God and have "fallen" to some lower place, so that now there is some kind of gap that has to be made up. Either we have to go to God, or he has to come to us and help us back up. And even if we say that he has come to us, going to him must at least be some sort of an option, something for which we must strive, at least for those who really want to, even if we can't make it without help, because the gap is still there. And thus it turns out that it is into this gap that we pour all our theological nonsense, all our investments in piety. We engage ourselves not in *bearing fruit* befitting repentance, because that after all is only secondary. First we have to get to God. And our theology becomes an excuse and our piety simply a stalling game.

If I read the Bible correctly, that is entirely the wrong picture. Our sin consists not in "falling down," but precisely in the attempt to climb up—the attempt to storm heaven. It consists in listening to the voice of the tempter, "You will be like God." We are not, we should realize, above putting even our theology and piety in the service of that temptation. And the point is that Advent is the cure for all that. It proclaims a God who comes to us, precisely to cure us of our attempt to ascend, to cure us of our pretentious piety and our excuse theology. It tells us to repent and get down to earth where we belong and be humans, not gods. It tells us that going to God isn't even an option for us. He has ruled that out forever. For *God* is the one who comes to us.

And what then shall we do? Bear fruits that befit repentance! That's the only thing there is to do. That is the only way to greet the God of Advent. He is coming. Your piety cannot affect that in the least. He is trampling out the vintage where the grapes of wrath are stored. Nothing you can do will alter that. He comes to you. You cannot go to him. That is precisely the glory of it, the gospel of it. You need not be a god, just a human to look after your fellow humans. "He who has two coats, let him share with him who has none; and he who has food, let him do likewise." For the Lord has come to us.

Sermon preached on December 12, 1967

He Who Is to Come

When John heard in prison what the Messiah was doing, he sent word by his disciples and said to him, "Are you the one who is to come, or are we to wait for another?" Jesus answered them, "Go and tell John what you hear and see: the blind receive their sight, the lame walk, the lepers are cleansed, the deaf hear, the dead are raised, and the poor have good news brought to them. And blessed is anyone who takes no offense at me."

As they went away, Jesus began to speak to the crowds about John: "What did you go out into the wilderness to look at? A reed shaken by the wind? What then did you go out to see? Someone dressed in soft robes? Look, those who wear soft robes are in royal palaces. What then did you go out to see? A prophet? Yes, I tell you, and more than a prophet. This is the one about whom it is written,

> *'See, I am sending my messenger ahead of you,*
> *who will prepare your way before you.'*

Truly I tell you, among those born of women no one has arisen greater than John the Baptist; yet the least in the kingdom of heaven is greater than he.

MATTHEW 11:2-11 NRSV

"Are you he who is to come, or shall we look for another?" There is, I think, almost a touch of despair in that question. Are you the one, or must it just go on and on and on, forever? Is there no end—or as we put it today, no finality, no uniqueness? Tell us, Jesus! Are you he, or shall we look for another?

"Well," we might ask, "who wants to know?" In our text, John the Baptist wants to know. John the Baptist? But I thought he knew! Is not he the one we have been hearing about these past weeks? Did he not leap in his mother's womb when Mary drew near? Didn't he say that he was unworthy to tie Jesus' shoe laces? That Jesus should baptize him rather than that he should baptize Jesus? Didn't he hear the voice from heaven? Didn't he point the finger and say, "Behold the Lamb of God?"

Well, perhaps. But apparently, in any case, it is not so easy as all that, not even for John. Because regardless of what he once knew, he still wants to know. And well he might, I suppose. John, the rock 'em, sock 'em, tell-it-like-it-is preacher of repentance. John, who had prophesied the big show, the ax laid to the root of the trees, the winnowing fork which will sift it all out at last, and the big fire that will burn away all the chaff and make things pure. And he got them all out there to the Jordan for the big baptism to protect them from the fire. Furthermore, for all his pains and protests he had finally gotten himself thrown in prison.

Well, *he* might ask, especially he, from his prison: "Are you he who is to come, or are we to look for another?" Show us your ID card, Jesus! Tell us so we don't have to go on and on and on. Tell us so that we don't miss it.

But the answer comes back: Well, it's just that the blind see, the lame walk, lepers are cleansed, the deaf hear, the dead are raised up, and the poor have good news preached to them. "And blessed the one who takes no offense at me."

Is that all? Yes, that's it. Just acts of mercy. Not much, perhaps. Unless, of course, you are deaf, or blind, or lame, or unclean, or dead, or poor. Then, I suppose, it would be quite a lot—maybe even everything. But then, not many of us are that, are we? So that's all there is—just acts of mercy. But where is the holocaust, where is the fire? How does that stack up with all that John had said? Unless, of course, those acts of mercy—unless that *was* the fire, burning, burning for us. I suppose John's problem was that after all he hadn't expected to get caught and sifted by that winnowing fork or burned by that fire! "Blessed the one," Jesus says, "who takes no offense at me!"

But now, what is all that to you? So what if John didn't know or wavered or was uncertain? Did you think to make hay out of John's doubt or trade on John's prestige or faith? What did you go out into the desert to see? A reed shaken by the wind? Someone blown this way and that by the hot winds of inspiration or the chill blasts of despair that afflict us all? Was that it? What did you expect to get from John? The assurance that all was well with us, that everything was going according to plan? A self-assured prestigious figure to lean on, a great man, perhaps, clothed in all the finery that human device can muster to mask its nakedness? Is that what you expected of John? Such people you will find only in king's houses, or houses of parliament, or even White Houses. If that is what you expected of John, you are playing the wrong game. For John was a prophet—indeed more than a prophet. For even if John didn't quite know, perhaps, what he was all about, *God* knows, and that is what finally matters. This is he, in spite all of the ills the flesh is heir to, of whom God said, "Behold, I send my messenger before thy face, who shall prepare thy way before thee." And we have no cause to lord it over him, because he is the best there is of our kind, the most one can expect of those born of woman, one whose life ends as an open question on the threshold of the Kingdom of heaven, the Kingdom of those and made new by the fire of pure, absolute mercy—where even the least is someone greater than John.

And so John's question becomes our question. Are you he who is to come, or shall we look for another? And perhaps for now, at least, we can do no better than to let the question stand and attend to the story that is about to unfold before us yet once more this year. The story which begins with the wail of an unwanted babe in the night, the story of one who insisted on being the *friend* of sinners, and ends with a cry of despair from the cross and the silence and darkness of the tomb—a silence and a darkness broken only for those who are not deaf to the song or blind to the light of Easter morning. He came once, and he is coming again this year and will come until the deaf hear, the blind see, the lame walk, the lepers are cleansed, the dead live, and the poor hear the good news at last. And blessed the one who takes no offence at him!

Let us pray:

> Ah dearest Jesus, Holy Child,
> Make thee a bed, soft, undefiled
> Within my heart, that it may be
> A quiet chamber kept for thee.

Come, Lord Jesus. Amen.

Sermon preached a Luther Seminary chapel, December 16, Third Sunday in Advent, 1974

And Lo, the Star

> *. . . and lo, the star which they had seen in the East went before them, till it came to rest over the place where the child was. When they saw the star, they rejoiced exceedingly with great joy, and going into the house they saw the child with Mary his mother, and they fell down and worshipped him.*
>
> MATTHEW 2:9-11 RSV

At this rather late date—when the trimmings of Christmas have been taken down, when the tree is chucked out in the back yard, and we are growing tired of eating left-over Christmas baking—it may seem strange to choose what we have come to think of as a Christmas text. However, to this several things can be said. First, according to the church, which as you know is just independent enough to operate on its own time-table, Christmas is not really over yet—not until tomorrow, for this is the twelfth day of Christmas. Second, these verses strictly speaking belong to the text for Epiphany, which is tomorrow, so actually I am a day early. And finally, and most important, it is not just out of a kind of perverse desire to drag things out that the church has seen fit to prolong the Christmas season and then to follow it with Epiphany; it is rather because there are more things to be said about Christmas, more things to be pondered than what can simply be crowded into a few days. Thus Christmas is followed by Epiphany—which means manifestation, a season in which heaven, for once, shows its hand, in which the darkness and gloom of earth is pierced for a fleeting moment and the light of eternity shows through.

Epiphany, the season of manifestation, stands under the sign of the star, the morning star, whose beams, as the hymn has it, are full of grace and truth. But now what about this star? Just what is its meaning? What does it intend to imply? I suppose if we look at it through the eyes of modern science it becomes something of a problem. Is it possible, in this twentieth century, when we are all aware of the fact that stars and heavenly bodies move according to fixed astronomical rules, that we are actually asked to base our faith on such strange goings-on? Is faith to be dependent on what some will call a bit of ancient astronomical folk lore? We are told that at the time of Christ such things were quite common, and that men searched the heavens for omens, for signs and portents, and that they believed that the destinies of men could be read from the movements of heavenly bodies. Is this what scripture intends us to believe? Is this the kind of stuff out of which faith is made? Some, apparently, would have us think so. But when we look at the interpretation of this passage in the tradition of the church, we find interestingly enough that the answer to this question is a resounding no! From the very beginning the fathers of the church interpreted this text to mean that with the appearance of Christ the time for such nonsense was over. They said that the purpose of the star was not to perpetuate a belief in the superstitions of astrology, but rather to bring them to an end. The time when men thought they could read their destiny from the stars had come to an end because the key to their destiny was born in the cradle at Bethlehem. The text itself indicates this by saying that the star went before them till it came to rest over the place where the child was. Here astrology and superstition come to an end; here the human search comes to an end. God is made manifest in the child; the light of eternity shines through in him.

Thus we find ourselves confronted by a rather strange paradox. If we today find it difficult to believe in the kind of astronomical phenomenon recorded in the text, this is due to the fact that it is the Christian faith itself which has taught us not to believe in such things. This is paradoxical but nevertheless true. But this paradox is not merely a contradiction, for hidden within it is a lesson on the nature of faith, a lesson in the meaning of Christmas and the mystery of the child's manifestation. His manifestation is good news. He comes not to add to the burden of superstition and fear, but to liberate from these things. His star is no ordinary star—it is not one which we need to worry about; it can take care of itself. And thus it is with this star. It stands always as a pointer, as an occasion for great rejoicing, and God forbid that we should ever turn it into a burden with which to tyrannize the minds of humans. It does not attract attention to itself; it is a sign, a sign of the fact that our quest is ended, that the time for fear and superstition is over. For when they saw this star, "they rejoiced exceedingly with great joy, and going into the house they saw the child with Mary his mother, and they fell down and worshipped him." It is not the purpose of this star to lead us into superstition and fear, nor into tracing the ways of the heavens—however worthy that may be—but to lead to him. Therefore we do not worry ourselves with speculations about it. We just let it shine in our darkness to lead us to him. And we say with the hymn writer,

> Brightest and best of the sons of the morning,
> Dawn on our darkness and lend us thine aid;
> Star of the east, the horizon adorning,
> Guide where our infant Redeemer is laid.

Healing

When he came down from the mountain, great crowds followed him; and behold, a leper came to him and knelt before him, saying, "Lord, if you will, you can make me clean." And he stretched out his hand and touched him, saying, "I will; be clean." And immediately his leprosy was cleansed. And Jesus said to him, "See that you say nothing to any one; but go, show yourself to the priest, and offer the gift that Moses commanded, for a proof to the people."

As he entered Caper'na-um, a centurion came forward to him, beseeching him and saying, "Lord, my servant is lying paralyzed at home, in terrible distress." And he said to him, "I will come and heal him." But the centurion answered him, "Lord, I am not worthy to have you come under my roof; but only say the word, and my servant will be healed. For I am a man under authority, with soldiers under me; and I say to one, 'Go,' and he goes, and to another, 'Come,' and he comes, and to my slave, 'Do this,' and he does it." When Jesus heard him, he marveled, and said to those who followed him, "Truly, I say to you, not even in Israel have I found such faith. I tell you, many will come from east and west and sit at table with Abraham, Isaac, and Jacob in the kingdom of heaven, while the sons of the kingdom will be thrown into the outer darkness; there men will weep and gnash their teeth." And to the centurion Jesus said, "Go; be it done for you as you have believed." And the servant was healed at that very moment.

MATTHEW 8:1-13 RSV

Our text for today, the account of the healing of a leper and of the centurion's servant, is one which is chosen to lead us farther and deeper into the manifestation of our Lord, into the showing-forth of what he really means for this world of ours. In this text he manifests himself in another dimension of human existence. The First Sunday after the Epiphany dealt with the child Jesus in the Temple, with childhood, parents, learning and things like that. The Second Sunday after the Epiphany dealt with the story of the wedding at Cana, a delightful story of the way in which our Lord manifested his glory in the joys of life at a marriage feast when the wine ran out. But life, of course, has other dimensions than these, and much as we might like to remain with these more pleasant things, especially when we are young, yet we must move on. So today we come to this account of the manner in which our Lord manifested himself in the darker dimensions of life, in the midst of human woe, misery, disease, and despair. This too is a part of life. This too cries out for a manifestation.

When he had come down from the mountain, our text says, great crowds followed him. "And behold, a leper came to him and knelt before him saying, 'Lord, if you will, you can make me clean.'" The mountain referred to is the one where Jesus had just finished preaching the Sermon on the Mount. Up there on the mountain he had spoken in terms of true obedience, of perfection, of the high and lofty ideals of the Kingdom of God—the kind of thing which has stirred men's hearts and appealed to their consciences ever since. Up there on the mountain he was a master teacher. It was a kind of classroom of his ministry. Some people seem to know and like only this Jesus of the mountainside, high above the ordinariness, the commonness, the problems, the repulsive diseases of humanity. And it seems they would just as soon that he stayed up there because everything else that he did is of little significance to them. So we hear it said, "I believe in the Sermon on the Mount—I don't know about all that other stuff, but the Sermon on the Mount is good enough for me." But Jesus, of course, did not stay up there on the mountain. He came down and was met by what we call the "stern realities" of life—the crowds with their smelly robes, their fickle dreams, their incessant clamoring and impetuous demands. He is met by the poor and, of course, the sick. But he does not hesitate. Here too he manifests his glory.

The healing of the leper gives us a graphic account of this manifestation, of the manner in which he takes these stern realities, this darker side of human existence, upon himself. Leprosy was, of course, the disease of diseases in Jesus' time. It was looked upon as having special religious implications as some sort of particular punishment from God, and the Hebrews regarded it with fear and awe. The leper was, I think we can say, religiously suspect; his disease was a symbol for sin and wretchedness. It was believed to be incurable, and anyone who had it could only hope for the special help of God. Thus the leper was an outcast, not only socially but religiously and ceremonially. He was unclean, and he had to live a life apart, according to strict rules and regulations so as not to contaminate others. If anyone came near, he was supposed to cry, "Unclean, unclean." People pulled away from him in fear and dread. Even the rabbis would have nothing to do with lepers most of the time. Some would hide themselves whenever they saw a leper coming. Some would even pelt them with stones, crying, "Away to thine own place, lest thou pollute others." They were cut off and, according to the Talmud, the interpretation of the law, they were reckoned as dead.

And now this leper, this untouchable, comes to Jesus, and Jesus stretches forth his hand and touches him. This was an extremely significant action on Jesus' part. It meant that he took the whole burden of the man's disease upon himself. He renders himself ceremonially unclean; he takes the contamination upon himself; he reaches out and touches the leper to draw him back into the land of the clean and the living. In our Old Testament lesson we heard the story of the cleansing of Naaman the Syrian by Elisha. But Elisha does not touch Naaman. As a matter of fact he will not even come out to see him. The early fathers of the church laid a good deal of stress on this difference and saw in it a sign of the perfection of the new covenant as over against the old. Perhaps this is reading a little much into the difference, but at any rate perhaps it does help to set forth the significance of Jesus' act. He comes down from the mountain and takes the risk, the weight of human disease and despair on himself.

In the second story in our text, the point is pretty much the same in spite of differences. To be sure, Jesus does not touch the centurion's servant. As a matter of fact, he does not even see him. This is one of the rare instances recorded in the gospels where a miracle is spoken of as being performed at a distance, without any contact with the person involved. But the point here is that the centurion is a Gentile. He too, like the leper, is one who is religiously under suspicion. He was, to the Jew, outside the scope of God's plans for God's chosen people. He had supposedly no right to claim Jesus' attention, no right to claim what was happening for himself. Nevertheless, Jesus did not hesitate. When asked, he says, "I will come and heal him." But even then the centurion is reluctant to impose. He says, "Lord, I am not worthy that you should come under my roof; but only say the word, and my servant will be healed. For I am a man under authority, with soldiers under me, and I say to one, 'Go,' and he goes, and to another, 'Come,' and he comes, and to my slave, 'Do this,' and he does it." The centurion is telling Jesus that as a Gentile he has no right to claim Jesus' presence, but that nevertheless he believes that Jesus has the authority to bring the disease to an end. He tells Jesus: I know what it is to command, all those under me must obey—so also the disease must obey you; only say the word. Jesus marvels at the man's faith and says, "Go; be it done for you as you as you have believed." Thus this healing story came to symbolize Jesus' manifestation to the Gentiles. Jesus does not go to the centurion's house. So also the Gentiles did not see nor receive Jesus according to the flesh, but nevertheless his healing power goes out to them as well through his word.

Thus in these stories, Jesus manifests his glory on the darker side of life. He meets the sick and the suffering with his healing touch and his saving word. But beyond that, I think these stories say even a little bit more. The persons involved, the leper and the centurion, were, as we have seen, religious outcasts. According to the official religion of the day they were ceremonially unclean, and they had no right, supposedly, to expect any kind of favors from the Jewish God. They didn't measure up; they were the kind who could just as well have told themselves, "After all, all this has nothing to do with us; religion is for nice people, for those who are clean and acceptable. Religion is for a select group, for the Jews, perhaps—or as we would say today, for the Christians." They were the kind in whom the organized religion as they knew it could only work despair because it was out of reach for them. There was too much to do, too many requirements which they couldn't hope to fulfill, too much to believe—and the official priests were always around ready to remind them of all this at the drop of a hat. The leper, for instance, had a whole array of rules he was supposed to live by, rules which no doubt would have forbidden his approach to Jesus had he carried them out to the letter. Religion could only mean despair for him. And it seems to me that we can detect a note of this despair in his plea as he kneels before Jesus: "Lord, if you will, you can make me clean." And Jesus reaches across the chasm, the great gulf of despair which separates them, and touches him. He reaches across all the rules, all the paraphernalia of religion; he sweeps them aside and heals. Out of man's despair he creates faith.

So I would like to look upon these texts as a manifestation of Jesus' power in the midst of man's despair. It may sound strange to say this when the centurion and the leper too are taken as examples of such great faith. But true faith and despair are very often closely related to one another. Luther always said this, when he looked back on his own anxiety. He said that true faith was born out of despair, when a person comes to that point where he despairs of himself, of his religion, of everything he has to offer God. Then he is at that point where God can do something with him. Many of you, no doubt, will experience times when the warmth, the inspiration you may have felt in your faith suddenly disappears. You wake up one morning and find that everything that you had taken for granted is vanished, and there is nothing left but a kind of void, a despair. And then all the official rules and prescriptions don't seem to do any good, and there is no method any more for getting back to what you have lost. But maybe when you have reached this stage, you have come to a point where God can do something at last, for then you can only look to him, like the leper and the centurion. For that is the way faith is born. It is born precisely out of despair. It is created by God when one despairs of finding any other way.

I think this is why Jesus commends the centurion's faith so highly. It was a faith born out of a great despair, the despair that he, a Gentile, could ever receive help. But its very helplessness was its strength. "Truly, I say to you, not even in Israel have I found such faith. I tell you, many will come from east and west and sit at table with Abraham, Isaac, and Jacob in the kingdom of heaven, while the sons of the kingdom will be thrown into the outer darkness; there men will weep and gnash their teeth." The implication seems to be that that kind of faith which is most assured of itself is most in danger of losing all. When one thinks that faith is something which one has in one's pocket, then one may be most in danger of losing it. For faith is not something that humans can produce. Faith comes when Jesus reaches across the chasm of despair and heals.

This is his manifestation to us, his epiphany to us today. He comes down from the mountain, he reaches out his hand, he sends forth his word to heal and to save. There is no barrier he cannot break down, no chasm he cannot cross. Jesus meets every request for help with a sure "I will." For these accounts of his healing are, according to the gospels, not really the half of it. They are but signs, indicators, clues of the kingdom which is breaking in in his person, signs of the greater manifestation, the greater epiphany in his cross and resurrection. There he takes the entire burden of our leprosy, our sin, our despair, even our rejection, upon himself and suffers it. And through this now he reaches out to touch us, in spite of everything, to heal, to say to us, "Be clean."

On the God-ness of God

The next day Jesus decided to go to Galilee. And he found Philip and said to him, "Follow me." Now Philip was from Bethsaida, the city of Andrew and Peter. Philip found Nathanael, and said to him, "We have found him of whom Moses in the law and also the prophets wrote, Jesus of Nazareth, the son of Joseph." Nathanael said to him, "Can anything good come out of Nazareth?" Philip said to him, "Come and see." Jesus saw Nathanael coming to him, and said of him, "Behold, an Israelite indeed, in whom is no guile!" Nathanael said to him, "How do you know me?" Jesus answered him, "Before Philip called you, when you were under the fig tree, I saw you." Nathanael answered him, "Rabbi, you are the Son of God! You are the King of Israel!" Jesus answered him, "Because I said to you, I saw you under the fig tree, do you believe? You shall see greater things than these." And he said to him, "Truly, truly, I say to you, you will see heaven opened, and the angels of God ascending and descending upon the Son of man."

JOHN 1:43-51 RSV

Beloved of God, called to be saints, grace to you and peace from God our Father and the Lord Jesus Christ!

The Roman Catholic theologian Harry McSorley in his book on Luther makes some telling remarks in criticism of the stance both Catholics and Protestants have come to adopt over against God's sovereignty, God's election, and God's predestination. "It is difficult to understand," he says, "how the Christian preacher can neglect to speak of election and calling when God has revealed himself as a God who elects and calls according as he pleases. Does one really believe in the mysterious God of the Old and New Testaments unless he believes in a God of election and predestination?"[3] And in another place he says, "One need only ask the average Catholic, or modern Protestant, a few questions concerning grace and predestination to discover that many of them—including those who have been catechized and preached to for years—have very little awareness of the absolute sovereignty of God's grace, and therefore of the mystery of God himself."[4]

Coming from a Roman Catholic, I think these are very interesting statements. They raise, I think, some rather embarrassing questions for us. Why is it that we hear so little about this God whom we find in the Bible? Granted, such things as God's sovereignty, election, and predestination are hard on us—things we find difficult to handle—and which have caused the church much difficulty throughout its history. Yet the fact remains that when you pick up the Bible, there it is! There you find that the God of whom the Bible speaks can virtually be identified by the fact that he is the God of election: He is the God who chose Abraham, Isaac, and Jacob, he is the God who chose Israel and guided her destiny—indeed arranged the destinies of all other nations so that they fit into the picture of Israel's destiny. He is the God who gave St. Paul the guts to address his congregation as those *called* of God from the beginning to be saints. That is the way the God of the Bible looks. Yet as we move about in the church, I think it safe to say that we don't really hear much about *this* God. We hear a lot, perhaps, about other kinds of Gods, but not *this* one! The God we usually hear about is, you might say, "Brand X," the "ordinary one," but not this specific, particular God.

So perhaps Father McSorley's question ought to be pressed: Why so little talk of this God? It is, I suppose, because we are afraid of him. God threatens us. He threatens to reduce us to insignificance. He does not really fit, I suppose, with what we like to call the modern consciousness of "freedom." We cannot really allow him to move too far into the center of the stage for fear he will seem to take too big a place. And I can imagine that even as I speak some of you are sort of half apprehensive about what I am going to say—that I might, perhaps, even be nervy enough to come out and actually say that

God predestines men, calls men, elects men to salvation! I suppose that would be a pretty chancy thing to say! We are nervous about this God—edgy. We would rather, I suppose, forget him; we would rather that the subject not even be brought up, and by a conspiracy of silence, allow him to slip into oblivion.

And thus a strange thing comes about. We call ourselves biblical Christians, but we don't really talk much about the God of the Bible. We hold him off at arm's length and make him into our celestial errand boy. Instead of being the God who elects us, he becomes the God who only "seconds" what we have elected to do. He is the *deus ex machina,* our need-fulfiller, our little "kept" God. And because we, who are supposed to be the proclaimers of the God of the Bible have by default, by our own conspiracy of silence, reduced him to this, there is small wonder, it seems to me, that there are rumors going around to the effect that God is dead.

Why are we afraid to speak about this God? Is not this fright, this nervousness we have about him rather ridiculous? Do we really believe that God is going to do the world harm by ruling too much or, perhaps, by making the wrong choices? Can we really go so far as to believe that the God who has revealed himself to us in Jesus Christ cannot be trusted with all that power so that we have, somehow, to cut him down to size? Are not all of our protestations in the end rather silly? What is there to be afraid of?

The little incident in the text from St. John's Gospel which we read for today is interesting, I think, in this light. Jesus calls Philip, and Philip brings Nathanael to Jesus. Jesus hails Nathanael with these words, "Behold, an Israelite indeed, in whom there is no guile"—a salutation which indicates that Jesus has more than ordinary information about what is going on. Nathanael is rather startled at all this and asks how Jesus came by this knowledge. And Jesus replies, "Before Philip called you, when you were under the fig tree, I saw you." Now if Nathanael had reacted to this as one of us "moderns," he would no doubt have said something like this, "Wait a minute! You mean to say you knew just what was going to happen? You mean to say that you were completely in control of the situation all the time? If that's the way it is, then I don't want to have anything to do with it!

After all, I have my dignity too. I don't want to play this game at all!" But Nathanael didn't say that. He said, "Rabbi, you are the Son of God! You are the King of Israel!" Nathanael knew God's action when he saw it. And then Jesus replies: That little bit about the fig tree was nothing. That was only the beginning. Stick around. You haven't seen anything yet. You will see the very heavens opened and angels ascending and descending upon the Son of man.

The point is that there is really nothing to fear. He has chosen you; fear not. If you let God be God, let him be the God he claims to be, then you will see great things. You will see the heavens opened and that great mystery which men seem so desperately to fear will be revealed. You will see God face to face.

Whoever Would Save His Life

For whoever would save his life will lose it; and whoever loses his life for my sake, he will save it.

LUKE 9:24 RSV

The road to life, the road that God gives, leads through death. This is the most difficult lesson of all for us to learn. It is difficult because we cling so tenaciously to our life, the life of the "Old Adam." We don't want to die, to surrender, to give it all up. We want to stay alive—and on our own terms. So we set up our little systems of meaning and morality so that we can convince ourselves, as we put it, "that life is worth living" on our own terms and cling to it. And sometimes, perhaps even more often than we think, we devise systems of theology which are really nothing but clever attempts to avoid dying. We try to make it appear even that God has entered the world in order to prop up our petty attempts to have life on our own terms.

This kind of theology can take many subtle forms. It may be that we want to preserve for ourselves that "little bit of responsibility" before God, as we so cleverly put it, so as to make sure that our destiny remains in our own hands. Or it may even be that we like to picture our faith in terms of heroic self-denial and sacrifice in obedience to some kind of standard, even the standard of the Bible. We prop up these standards with all sorts of theories about their authority and sublimity, and then we bow before them. We are willing, perhaps, even to pay a high price, to shut out all the "voices of worldly reason" and science, to sacrifice even our intellect and style ourselves "true believers." But it is not necessarily dying. It may only be a desperate attempt to cling to life on our own terms.

And at this late date in the history of our tired world, it is becoming apparent that we can't get away with it anymore. We in the church, who are to preach the gospel of Jesus Christ ought to be crystal clear on that point. We do ourselves and the world no good at all by preaching a message which is nothing but a watered-down and pitiful attempt to applaud man's desire to have life on his own terms. For the sharp-eyed world sees through this subterfuge. The only ones we fool are ourselves. More and more voices are being raised which say that life is absurd and meaningless, and when we immediately become upset, and stamp our feet like disappointed children, and say, "It's not true; there is *so* a meaning to life," the world sees that we have put ourselves on the wrong side. When we are told that the morality of man is in a general state of collapse, and we rush like pious policemen to tell men that they must be good, the world finds us out.

To be sure, we have a responsibility in the search for meaning, and we have a responsibility for morality in the world. But we forget that we also have the responsibility of telling the world that it cannot find these things on its own. In our haste to prop up the world's collapsing enterprises, we unwittingly place ourselves on the wrong side. We become isolated little preserves for perpetuating the world's idle dreams, the last outposts in a lost cause. For what these voices that are becoming louder and louder are telling us is something which we should have known all along: There is no self-evident meaning to the world, and man's morality is more often than not a hoax. Apart from Christ there is absolutely no way out. Our Lord has said, "Whoever would save his life will lose it." The desperate attempts to have life on our own terms leads only to either despair or presumption, and in either case we lose—everything.

For why should we be afraid? Why should we be afraid to die this death? Why should we cling so tenaciously to this life and its follies? It is natural, of course, not to want to die, especially if you do not know or cannot trust in what death will bring. The Old Adam fights constantly for his life. Even those in the world who have seen some of the truth—our contemporary existentialists who have seen that life is absurd—even they do not finally have the courage to die this death. They must say that in spite of the painful conclusion that life is absurd, we must grit our teeth and go on. We must turn our backs and *decide* to be what we are; we must in effect become our own creators. So the existentialist *creates himself* "out of nothing" by his "decision" because he does not have the courage to die. What he has done is nothing more or less than to expose both the fear and the folly of the Old Adam, the gnawing fear that there is no meaning, but also the folly that he can create one for himself because he cannot die.

But why should *we* fear? It is understandable perhaps in the world. But why should we hold back and compromise and water down the message? We have a Lord who says, "Fear not!" "He who loses his life for my sake shall find it." We have a Lord who had the courage to die. And he died "in our place." He was not afraid to pass through the narrowness of death, and because of this he won the crown of life. We need not fear this death—death to the self, to the Old Adam and its anxious attempts to have life on its own terms, this death to the world and its frantic efforts to create life and its fruitless search for meaning. We need not fear that death. We need not fear giving ourselves to him, for he died and showed us that *life*—the life that God has to give—waits for us. He has promised, "Whoever loses his life for my sake, he will save it."

And if we have died in him, we cannot compromise this message, this gospel, in our ministry to the world. To do so is to do the world the greatest disservice. For we must tell the world that in order to have life, it must die. We cannot make it seem as though faith is merely another of the world's attempts to escape dying. For the faith we preach, if it is anything at all, is dying—dying to the world to live to God. For we preach a Lord who came to die. We preach a Lord who in the night in which he was betrayed, when he was about to be crushed by this world's attempts to create life, steadfastly took the cup and said in effect, "I have a cup of which I must drink, and you too must drink of it, all of you. For this is the *new testament,* the new covenant, the covenant of my death and resurrection." Life on God's terms comes through his death. And faith is dying, dying to have life. And if we have died, then—and only then—we can go on to speak of meaning and morality—on God's terms. "For whoever would save his life will lose it; and whoever loses his life for my sake, he will save it."

Sermon preached at Luther Seminary Chapel, February 22, 1965

Sin and Grace

What shall we say then? Are we to continue in sin that grace may abound? By no means! How can we who died to sin still live in it? Do you not know that all of us who have been baptized into Christ Jesus were baptized into his death? We were buried therefore with him by baptism into death, so that as Christ was raised from the dead by the glory of the Father, we too might walk in newness of life.

For if we have been united with him in a death like his, we shall certainly be united with him in a resurrection like his. We know that our old self was crucified with him so that the sinful body might be destroyed, and we might no longer be enslaved to sin. For he who has died is freed from sin. But if we have died with Christ, we believe that we shall also live with him. For we know that Christ being raised from the dead will never die again; death no longer has dominion over him. The death he died he died to sin, once for all, but the life he lives he lives to God. So you also must consider yourselves dead to sin and alive to God in Christ Jesus.

ROMANS 6:1-11 RSV

"What shall we say then? Are we to continue in sin that grace may abound?" What a dangerous, disquieting question! What does Paul mean by injecting it into our relatively complacent and smug lives? Who is this "troubler of Israel"? What shall we do with such an "unorthodox" if not "heretical" question?

There are at least two ways, I think, in which we might react to the question. The first and perhaps most immediate would be what might be called a reaction "of the right," a kind of "knee-jerk" reaction, one of shocked, if not offended disavowal, a reaction reflecting a certain complacency about grace. Shall we sin the more that grace may abound? Of course not! My goodness! Doesn't Paul know that we are Christians, good, pious, law-abiding folks? Not to say seminarians and seminary professors to boot? Surely Paul must not be serious. The question must surely be just a rhetorical one! How could we even entertain such a shocking thought? We are afraid even to let the question arise. It offends and turns us back, back to our old self-satisfied and self-assured ways. With righteous zeal and posturing of one sort or another we pick up the trumpets, hoist the banners, and march off to do battle, perhaps in the name of morality and decency, lustily singing "Onward Christian soldiers, marching as to war," entirely oblivious of the fact that we may actually be in full retreat! Because we haven't really heard the question or grasped its serious intent. And because we haven't heard the question, we never hear the answer.

But the second reaction might be equally presumptuous, a reaction "on the left," which reflects a certain complacency about sin. Shall we continue in sin that grace may abound? Why not? Is it not, after all, God's business to be gracious? Besides, what harm does it do—as long as we are careful about it, and private enough so that "others" are not hurt by it in this so-called "permissive" age? Oh, of course, there may be some sins—injustices, perhaps—that we might get upset about, but they turn out for the most part to be the sins of others, usually against what we have come to term our "rights." In this case we are willing to entertain and flirt with the question, perhaps, but we never get much further. And so again we don't hear what Paul goes on to say. We supply our own answer. We don't hear the "By no means!" Or as we might put it in a more contemporary idiom: No way!

But why then does Paul put the question? Why does he flirt so dangerously on the brink of disaster? It is, I expect, because Paul knows that the question is not merely a rhetorical one; it is a question which must be put, must be hurled into the midst of our complacency and smug self-centeredness, all the pious rhetoric on both the right and the left—a question which attacks both our complacency about grace and our complacency about sin, for those are really just variations on the same theme, our own pet causes. The question must be put because anyone who knows anything about grace, anyone who has followed the argument to this point in the epistle, knows that it is God's last wild gamble to get us and save us. The question pushes us to the farthest dangerous extremity of our thinking in this evil and adulterous age, and unless it is put and really heard, we shall never know that there is something *on the other side,* something utterly new!

But, but, don't we *have to* do something, at least some little thing? That is the form in which the question usually arises among us, I suppose. How like us in our last extremity to cry out thus when we have been exposed for what we are, suddenly to get all pious about that little bit we had planned to get away with! The question is no doubt a sign that the message is getting to us and we tremble—on the brink of freedom. For you see, that question—don't we *have to* do something?—is not the question at all any longer. The question now is, what *are* you going to do now that you don't *have to* do anything? It is an entirely new ball game, for the grace of God has come. Jesus has been raised from the dead!

Why does Paul put the question? Because it is the only question left to ask—in order that the answer, God's answer, may be heard somehow above the din of our protestation, in order that we might be able to get a glimpse of something that's even more exciting than sin! So perk up your ears and listen! "Shall we continue in sin that grace may abound? By no means! How can we who have died to sin still live in it? Do you not know that all of us who have been baptized into Christ Jesus have been baptized into his death? We were buried therefore with him by baptism into death, so that as Christ was raised from the dead by the glory of the Father, we too might walk in newness of life." Christ has been raised from the dead. It's an entirely new ball game! Nothing else, but nothing! matters now.

Of course our battle is not over. Let us not deceive ourselves. We will sin. Paul certainly knows that well; see the next chapter of Romans! We will sin, and grace will nevertheless abound. But our sin and God's grace can never now be connected by an "in order that."

Sin and Grace | 49

A death has intervened. Our sin drove Jesus to the cross and the grave once—but no more. God raised him up. Our battle is not over, but God's is! Grace will abound! For we know that Christ being raised from the dead will never die again, death no longer has dominion over him. The death he died he died to sin *once for all,* but the life he lives, he lives to God. God's action is irreversible! Let not sin reign, for you are not under law but under grace!

So let there finally be an end to all the posturing and rhetoric on the right and on the left. For if we have been united with him in a death like his, we shall certainly be united with him in a resurrection like his. One who has died is freed from sin. So you, dear hearers, you also, must consider yourselves dead to sin and alive to God in Christ Jesus.

For to Me to Live Is Christ

For to me to live is Christ, and to die is gain.

PHILIPPIANS 1:21 RSV

Bertrand Russell, in an essay entitled "Why I am *not* a Christian," states that one of his reasons for rejecting Christianity is that religion is, after all, based on fear. "Religion," he says, "is based primarily and mainly upon fear. It is partly the terror of the unknown, and partly . . . the wish to feel that you have a kind of elder brother who will stand by you in all your troubles and disputes. Fear is the basis of the whole thing—fear of the mysterious, fear of defeat, fear of death." Religion, in Mr. Russell's view, feeds on man's weaknesses. It is man's attempt to wrap a kind of protective covering around himself, to enable him to live in this world which is so inhospitable and keep a sense of well-being—perhaps even to enable him to keep his sanity. Religion is a detour, because if man takes the path of religion he is slow to face his real problems and solve them with good English common sense. It is a kind of womb, we might say, which man refuses to leave, because he is afraid.

But now, when I take this statement of Mr. Russell's and compare it with the statement of St. Paul which we read, I am led to wonder if they are really talking about the same thing at all. St. Paul says, "For to me to live is Christ, and to die is gain." I must confess that this statement is one which has always made me a little uneasy. And I think what makes me uneasy about it is its utter candor and fearlessness. How can he say it? How can he say that Christ is after all the entire meaning of life for him and that death is no real worry? The answer lies of course in the fact that something has happened in Paul's life which made the whole question of fear suddenly irrelevant. Paul had been claimed by Christ. It was not, he tells us, that he hadn't been religious—he had been overly so. It was not that he was looking for something to calm his fears even. It was simply the fact that one fine day he had been claimed by Christ, and that had made all the difference. He did not choose it. He was not shopping for a religion—as though it were a matter of looking over the alternatives and then picking the one he could be most comfortable with. But Christ chose him, and that was the end of the matter. And when he tries to describe what it was like, he says it was like dying, and all the fears which he had "in the flesh," as he put it, died too. In Christ he was reborn, created anew, and placed in the world to follow Christ, come what may.

Therefore he can say that to live is Christ and to die is gain. And he goes on in this passage, writing from prison where the possibility of death was near, to talk about his own living or dying with utter candor. "Which I shall choose," he says, "I cannot tell. I am hard pressed between the two. My desire is to depart and be with Christ, for that is far better. But to remain in the flesh is more necessary on your account. Convinced of this, I know that I shall remain and continue with you all, for your progress and joy in the faith, so that in me you may have ample cause to glory in Christ Jesus, because of my coming to you again." For Paul, the problem of fear, at least the kind of fear that Mr. Russell is talking about, seems rather irrelevant.

So I wonder if we can't say that it may well be true that *religion* is based on fear—I don't know whether this is so or not. That is a question that we can leave for the anthropologists and psychologists to argue about. But this has little or nothing to do with the Gospel of Jesus Christ. Granted we all have our fears—fear of the mysterious, fear of defeat, fear of death—and there is enough truth in what Mr. Russell says to give us cause to stop and think. But God in Christ calls us to a different kind of life. He calls us out of fear to a life which is beyond even the question, a life in which the entire issue is forgotten. Christ did not come to hold us in a state of perpetual fear so that we will feel the need of him only to the degree to which we are afraid. He came to set us free from all that—to set us free even from the burden of religion. He came so that we could walk in joy and peace and enter into life in all its fullness. The angel who announced his birth said, "*Fear not*, for behold I bring you glad tidings of a great joy;

for unto you is born this day *a savior"*—not a new doctor of religion, but a savior. Fear is transcended, and peace and joy are restored to us. This is what God has done for us in Christ. It is a great gift, and to him belong all honor and praise and glory.

> Keep, we beseech thee, O Lord, thy church with thy perpetual mercy; and because the frailty of man without thee cannot but fall, keep us ever by thy help from all things hurtful, and lead us to all things profitable to our salvation; through thy Son, Jesus Christ our Lord who liveth and reigneth with thee and the Holy Ghost, one God, world without end. Amen.

Sermon preached at Luther College chapel, September 27, 1962

For God So Loved the World

> *For God so loved the world that he gave his only Son, that whoever believes in him should not perish but have eternal life. For God sent the Son into the world, not to condemn the world, but that the world might be saved through him.*
>
> JOHN 3:16-17 RSV

Saturday I was listening to the opera *Salome* which, as you recall, is based on the story of the beheading of John the Baptist. In it there is a scene in which some of the disciples of Jesus appear and tell Herod of the signs and wonders which are being performed by Jesus in fulfillment of the Baptist's prophecy. Herod, who is engaged in the grim business of getting rid of John, cries out, "I forbid him to do that!" Herod's exclamation set me to thinking—thinking that perhaps one of the things that bothers us most about the kind of God we find in the New Testament is his goodness—not the strictness or rules and regulations, but rather the sheer goodness and liberality of God. Herod's kingdom, which operated according to rules which he controlled and administrated was threatened by God's goodness being manifested in Christ, and Herod didn't like it, so he tried to put a stop to it.

And it seems to me that Herod's reaction reflects in a very real sense a reaction which is common to mankind. We like to enclose ourselves in cozy little kingdoms which run according to rules and regulations which we have set down and which we can understand, so that we can predict and pass judgment over what can and cannot happen. Certainly much of our thinking is directed toward that end. The old scientific ethos of the past two centuries which still hangs on today was driven partly by a desire to banish all mystery and uncertainty from our "Kingdom" so that we could rule it without interference. It brought us many good things, to be sure, things with which we do not want to part, but also in many instances it was misused in an attempt to put restrictions on God's goodness—in an attempt, so to speak, to put a cover on our world, to say of God's revelation in Christ, of his wonders, of his resurrection, "It can't happen"—to say, like Herod, "I forbid him to do that!"

But if this is true of such areas of thinking, it is no less true even of our thinking about religion—of our theology. As a human activity—and theology is a human activity—it too does not escape the ambitions of its Herods either. We develop all sorts of theological "isms," and we like to sit around and argue about how much or how little has to be believed. We argue about fundamentalism and liberalism and such dreary things. We like to establish rules and regulations according to which the Kingdom of God is supposed to be administrated. Of course there is a sense in which rules and regulations are necessary, but sometimes we become preoccupied with them and so impressed with our arguments about them that before we know it we have begun to restrict God's goodness—virtually to forbid him to act in any other way.

The text which we read for today, one which ought to be seared into the memory of every Christian, reminds us that God's goodness knows no bounds: "For God so loved the world that he gave his only Son, that whoever believes in him should not perish but have eternal life." God breaks through the limitations of this world, through his act in Christ. The thing which we have to guard against is the attempt on the part of men to restrict God's goodness. This is what theology ought to be about. As a Christian church we have only one thing basically to conserve: the message about God's goodness, God's liberality in Christ.

The charge is often made that Christianity is narrow minded. This is not so. On the contrary, this is a charge which ought to be made from the point of the Christian message against the world. The trouble with men's "isms" including those which pretend to be most "liberal" is that they usually hide attempts like Herod's to put limits on God's goodness and liberality. In some subtle way they impose a law upon man, which in the end will destroy him. But God, our text says, does not operate that way. He did not send his Son into the world to condemn the world, but that the world might be saved through him. His goodness in Christ knows no bounds. This is something we ought never to forget; and whatever we do, whatever we say ought always to be guided by the fact that we have only one thing to preserve, only one thing to bear witness to—God's liberality, God's goodness in Christ.

Give Thanks to the Lord

O give thanks to the Lord, for he is good; for his steadfast love endures forever!"

PSALM 106:1 NRSV

Thanksgiving vacation being just around the corner, this is the time of year when we focus our attention especially on the matter of giving thanks. So my talk for today shall consist of a few thoughts on that subject.

Giving thanks, it seems to me, is a posture which is strange to us so-called modern people. Perhaps it has always been so to a certain extent, but somehow I get the feeling that it is especially strange to us. To bow one's head for instance and give thanks for the food we eat is embarrassing for many. We squirm a little when the time for the Thanksgiving sermon rolls around and we are given our talking to for not being thankful enough. Usually we are treated to a nice long list of things which we have to be thankful for, as though we should talk ourselves into the posture of thankfulness once again. But we are all so used to these things, and we know that they are going to be there anyway, even if we don't give thanks. Thanksgiving is a strange posture for us to adopt.

I wonder sometimes why this is. Maybe a part of the reason is that we really have come to think that we are pretty good at providing things ourselves. We have developed something of a split vision. Inwardly we question just who it is or what we have to thank. We have grown so used to the idea of being "self-made," we spend so much time thinking about ourselves and our earning power that we find little place for God in all this. Our blessings, we are told over and over again, are the result of our system—economic and political, and it is "as Americans that we have so much to be thankful for." One gets the impression that we are really paying ourselves a compliment for being so clever and only incidentally thanking God for adding his stamp of approval on our industry and our schemes.

An interesting example of this split vision was an ad which appeared in one of the latest editions of *Time* magazine. The picture, a Norman Rockwell drawing, shows a family with bowed heads seated around the table on which the Thanksgiving feast is spread. The caption reads as follows: "At certain times of the year we're reminded how well off we are—as Americans. The most heartfelt thanks of all often come from the head of the table—especially these days when being a family provider is no light responsibility. For past blessings, it's a time for gratitude. For the future, a time for high hopes and careful planning." And then at the bottom of the page: "Massachusetts Mutual Life Insurance Company, Springfield, Massachusetts, organized 1851." One wonders what the point of it all is. Are they praying to God or to the insurance company? At any rate I don't think there is much doubt as to the reason why such an ad should appear. I doubt rather strongly that its purpose is to encourage people to give thanks to God. We develop a split vision, and we think that really we're pretty good after all.

But why should we give thanks? Is it because we have plenty? This could be taken away. Is it because we are Americans? This may be only conceit. Because of our economics, or even our insurance? These may only insulate us from the real truth about ourselves. All of these things, though we should ultimately give thanks for them too, are not the primary reasons for doing so. If they were, then we should cease to give thanks if they were gone. The psalmist in our text gives a different reason. He says, "O give thanks to the Lord, for he is good; for his steadfast love endures forever." This is fundamentally a different starting point. Instead of fixing our gaze first of all on ourselves and asking, "Let me see now, what is it I have to be thankful for this year?" we begin with God and his goodness. When we start here, we see that we in fact are not good and that we deserve only his wrath and destruction. When we start here we see that we exist at all only because of his mercy.

Everything we have, be it great or small, is in fact a gift of his grace, and every gift we receive is a mystery for which we should give thanks. We should thank him for the fact that he allows us to live even though we have broken the unity and harmony of creation. We cannot eat without cutting up, crushing, breaking down, and killing other creatures. Sometimes even the lives of our fellow men are sacrificed in this process. For this we all share the guilt. We should not sit down to partake of a meal without thanking him for allowing us to do so. We should thank him that he sustains us even though we make a mess of things. We cannot maintain order and justice and peace without creating misery and hatred and even killing some of our brothers. For this we all bear the guilt. We should give thanks that he preserves us nevertheless. We tear up the face of the earth, searching for things to sustain us. We destroy, break, betray, soil, pollute. But he is good and his mercy endures forever. He does not betray us, nor does his creation betray us—he lets us live. For this we owe him thanks. Knowing what we are, and what he is, this is the only attitude we can adopt toward him.

And this, of course, is only part of the story. For in his endless mercy, he not only allows us to live, he comes to us himself as one of us to redeem us. We treat him too like we treat his creation—we betray him. But he bears it, and out of this even, he brings forth something good—the greatest good of all—forgiveness and salvation. "O give thanks to the Lord, for he is good; for his steadfast love endures forever." Amen.

Sermon preached at Luther Seminary chapel

Loose Ends?

> *Awesome things will you show us in your righteousness, O God of our salvation, O hope of all the ends of the earth and of the seas that are far away.*
>
> PSALM 65:5 (from *Lutheran Book of Worship*)

We recite these words dutifully as part of our litany every time we do Responsive Prayer One, as it is rather inelegantly called, and as we are about to do again this morning. I don't know about you, but I get a kind of charge in my theological funny bone whenever I am actually paying attention to what is going on and not champing at the bit because we have already run overtime. "O hope of all the ends of the earth and of the seas that are far away?" Really? Did you ever hear of anything so delightfully irrelevant in this day and age? I would guess that the ends of the earth and the seas that are far away would hardly turn up very high on contemporary prayer lists. But here they are, right in the middle of lots of nice pious prayer about ourselves. (Indeed, one translator apparently thought it pointless to pray for the seas that are far away and changed it to read "and for *them* that are far off *upon* the sea"!) So I thought it might be well to reflect on these words just a little—hoping that just a little reflection won't spoil them. It's probably the kind of thing you don't want to think about too much.

What are we talking about here? "The ends of the earth and the seas that are far away"? I suppose the author really didn't know. And that, no doubt, is just the point. The ends, you might say, were pretty loose. And loose ends can be threatening. Somebody's got to care about the loose ends. There has to be some hope. And so the psalmist appeals to God, the God of our salvation, and waits for "awesome things." (In the Revised Standard Version: "By dread deeds thou dost answer us with deliverance.") The words were written, I expect, in the days when it was thought that the earth was flat and surrounded by angry seas. One could, theoretically at least, reach the ends of the earth. Not that anyone wanted to, because you might fall off and never come back. Or the ends that were far away could suddenly come near and come crashing in upon us. It could be a fearsome thing—the ends of the earth and the seas that are far away. God was the only hope.

But now, or course, we have learned better. The earth is round and whatever seas there are are not very far away. We fly over them in a matter of hours. They may still need hope, but only because they are in danger of being polluted. Since the earth is round, there are no ends. Now I'm no advocate of the flat earth society, but did you ever think how boring it is? Round? And we have been going around in circles ever since. We even have hymns to the "Eternal Ruler of the ceaseless round!" Boring! Is that one reason, perhaps, why we peer anxiously into space and launch our magnificently expensive but somehow insignificant puny probes into outer space? What are we looking for? Ends? Beginnings and endings? Some clue to how we got here and whither we are hasting? I saw the other day in the paper that NASA is now spending millions conducting an exhaustive scanning of space in this year of Columbus for radio waves that might indicate intelligent life out there. Is there someone out there? Is there any hope? And if there is, do you suppose they care? Can we ever reach them? Are we about to be colonized by some superior race? Wouldn't that be a fitting conclusion to the year of Columbus?

"O hope of all the ends of the earth, and of the seas that are far away"? Are they still there, those loose ends and those far away seas? Are we drifting toward some end? A random collision, a heat death, a black hole? Are we already in one—a space tunnel or worm? Will the cosmic seas wash in upon us when we have used up the ozone layer? Loose ends.

But now I am getting too heavy, thinking too much about it, perhaps. For the real point is that the God who is the hope of all the ends of the earth and of the seas that are far away has taken time out from a very busy agenda to drop in upon us, so to speak, to tie up at least one loose end, and to be the God of our salvation. And what is awesome about it is that once again you meet your end here and now. God is for you in Jesus and will take care. So we can pray over against all the loose ends and threatening seas: "Awesome things you will show us in your righteousness, O God of our salvation, O hope of all the ends of the earth, and of the seas that are far away!" Yes and amen.

Sermon preached at Luther Seminary chapel, October 22, 1992

Good and Evil

> *When the unclean spirit has gone out of a man, he passes through waterless places seeking rest; and finding none he says, "I will return to my house from which I came." And when he comes he finds it swept and put in order. Then he goes and brings seven other spirits more evil than himself, and they enter and dwell there; and the last state of that man becomes worse than the first.*
>
> LUKE 11:24-26 RSV

My talk this morning consists of a few thoughts on an old formula, often used by the fathers of the church: Evil is the absence of the good. As you may recall from your history of thought, this formula was used to solve the problem of the dualism of good and evil. Evil, they said, is not a positive power existing in its own right, it is simply negative—the absence of the good. And the formula was often criticized because, it is said, evil has more power than that, more power than mere absence or negation. And perhaps that is right. But I don't wish today to become involved in that metaphysical argument. I would like to consider whether the old formula does not have, after all, some more immediate and practical significance, especially against the background of the passage we have heard from St. Luke's gospel, where the unclean spirit, finding his former home vacant and swept clean, empty, brings seven more evil spirits back with him to dwell there. Evil is the absence of the good. Where there is no positive goodness, no real and concrete good action, *there* is evil, there the demons enter and have a field-day!

You see, it seems to me that in our pietistic tradition we have tended somehow to reverse the formula. We have tended to say that good is the absence of evil—that if we manage somehow simply to avoid evil, if we keep our houses swept clean, then we are, supposedly, by that very fact, good. You don't really have to do anything actually; you simply have to avoid doing a lot of evil things. For good, we tend to think, is the absence of evil. But this reversal of the formula can only have disastrous consequences. It can only lead, as I am afraid it does too much among us, to a stultifying ethic of conformity. We do not look for the real signs of positive creative goodness or activity either in ourselves or in our fellow men, we look only for the absence of a whole set of assumed evils. And that goes too for a whole set of supposed social evils which make a person of the type that doesn't really "fit in" with our cozy little group. We can't really take the person who is a little bit "kooky," the person who doesn't avoid our assumed set of evils—no matter how much creative and tempestuous, perhaps even impetuous goodness there may be in him—because we have consciously or unconsciously reversed the formula. Good is the absence of evil. So we value conformity before creativity, accommodation before sincerity and forthrightness. You don't even have to do honest, to say nothing of creative, work in your studies. Just avoid the evils the group has decreed, turn on the saccharine smile, and don't bother anyone, don't upset them, don't disagree, even if you feel you should, and you'll "get by." Just be "nice."

But I suggest that there was practical wisdom in the old formula. For mere absence of evil does not make good, but rather evil is the absence of the good. Where there is no positive good, no creative action, no actual doing of something, there is evil. For when the house is empty and vacuous, you can be certain the demons will find a way to return, and the last state of that man will be worse than the first. For really, we can take a lot of kookiness if there is something really doing; we can bear with a lot of sins if something positive is being accomplished. As our Lord once put it, "Where there is much love, much can be forgiven." But we really can't live long in the arid and vacuous desert where the mere absence of evil is equated with the good.

And certainly that is something of what the gospel is all about. For if Christ comes really to set us free, it is pretty difficult to see how that could result in stultifying conformity. If Christ came to set us free, that should result in the positive goodness of actually doing something. For only then will evil begin to lose the battle.

Sermon preached at Luther Seminary Chapel, January 17, 1967

On Sin

The Lord God took the man and put him in the garden of Eden to till it and keep it. And the Lord God commanded the man, "You may freely eat of every tree of the garden; but of the tree of the knowledge of good and evil you shall not eat, for in the day that you eat of it you shall die."

Now the serpent was more crafty than any other wild animal that the Lord God had made. He said to the woman, "Did God say, 'You shall not eat from any tree in the garden'?" The woman said to the serpent, "We may eat of the fruit of the trees in the garden; but God said, 'You shall not eat of the fruit of the tree that is in the middle of the garden, nor shall you touch it, or you shall die.'" But the serpent said to the woman, "You will not die; for God knows that when you eat of it your eyes will be opened, and you will be like God, knowing good and evil." So when the woman saw that the tree was good for food, and that it was a delight to the eyes, and that the tree was to be desired to make one wise, she took of its fruit and ate; and she also gave some to her husband, who was with her, and he ate. Then the eyes of both were opened, and they knew that they were naked; and they sewed fig leaves together and made loincloths for themselves.

They heard the sound of the Lord God walking in the garden at the time of the evening breeze, and the man and his wife hid themselves from the presence of the Lord God among the trees of the garden. But the Lord God called to the man, and said to him, "Where are you?" He said, "I heard the sound of you in the garden, and I was afraid, because I was naked; and I hid myself." He said, "Who told you that you were

> *naked? Have you eaten from the tree of which I commanded you not to eat?" The man said, "The woman whom you gave to be with me, she gave me fruit from the tree, and I ate." Then the Lord God said to the woman, "What is this that you have done?" The woman said, "The serpent tricked me, and I ate."*

GENESIS 2:15-17; 3:1-13 NRSV

It is traditional on this First Sunday in Lent, as our texts indicate, to be concerned about the problem of temptation and sin. The Gospel text (Matthew 4:1-11) tells the story of the temptation of Christ, the story of the victory of the second Adam over sin. The text which I have read from the Old Testament tells the story of the temptation of the first Adam, which resulted, as we all know, not in victory, but in some sort of defeat. What I would like to do this morning first of all is to go back to that story of the first Adam. I would like to do that because I would like you to reflect with me today on the question of sin, the question of our sin. In Lent we are concerned with the call to repentance. Perhaps it is well, therefore, that we ponder the question of our sin so that we are clear as to just what we have to repent of.

What is sin? How are we to understand it? I would like to begin today in perhaps an unconventional way by saying that it seems to me that in many ways the view of sin which has been and still is generally current among us is on the one hand unduly harsh and pessimistic, and on the other hand not very profound. It may be, even, that these two judgments are related—that we make up for the lack of profundity in our understanding of sin by harshness and pessimism. It is as though we have to convince ourselves that we really take sin seriously, as the saying goes, by being as hard on ourselves as we possibly can! But that's really not very profound. It's really only a kind of spiritual masochism, a self-flagellation. Furthermore, what is more serious, we run the risk of blaspheming against God the creator. In running ourselves down we might also be destroying the belief in the goodness of creation.

I don't know how you feel, but more and more I cringe when I get to that point in our regular liturgy where we confess ourselves to be "by *nature* sinful and unclean." I think I know what that means and I think I know why we have insisted theologically on saying it that way, but still I wonder if such phrases, in our day, don't do more harm than good because we really don't understand the subtleties of that kind of language any more. It seems, I think, almost as if we were saying that the very stuff we are made of is sinful. And, quite frankly, I cringe too at the words of some of our hymns—for instance when we sing lustily that we are "wounded, impotent, and blind!" It's almost as though we are willing to admit that God is pretty good at redemption but that he was really something of a flop at creation. Something in me rebels against certain kinds of "wounded, impotent, and blind" theology. It seems to me that it is a kind of theology that can make God and his grace look good and desirable only by making man look bad.

Of course I realize it might be dangerous to say things like that. For when I rebel at these views I must always ask myself why. Might it not be simply because of pride, because I don't really want to confess my sin? Might it not be that in talking about temptation I succumb to the temptation to make light of sin myself? It might be, of course. That is a possibility that must always be reckoned with. But I don't really think that's the case—at least I hope not. I rebel against such a view of sin because it doesn't really fit the case. In the end it does not do justice either to my belief in the goodness of creation nor to the seriousness of sin. In a real sense sin is more serious than our usual view lets on—so serious that no amount of brow beating will really make us own up to it, so serious that we can't expose it merely by the simple expedient of saying the worst things about ourselves we can think of. All that is merely playing with words—a game we use to cover up rather than expose the truth, a kind of false modesty which most people refuse to believe anyway and no one really takes seriously.

But why do we get into this kind of trouble over the doctrine of sin? I suppose there are a lot of reasons for it. But one of the chief reasons, I think, is the way we usually interpret the story of the "fall" of Adam. When we try to make sense of this story, it usually turns out something as follows: We call what happened to Adam a "fall." But what does that mean? A fall from what? And to what? The very idea of a fall implies that the "first Adam" started out somewhere higher up and then fell to a lower level—the level, apparently, where we, his "children," now find ourselves. The whole idea implies, we might say, something like a ladder of salvation. Adam started out at or at least near the top and then fell down and stuck us with the job of climbing back up.

Now it is precisely this kind of picture that gets us into all kinds of trouble. We are all well aware, of course, that it gets us into trouble with the scientists, especially the biological scientists. The very idea that man started out from some sort of original perfection is difficult to hold today. But we needn't dwell on that difficulty now. What we fail to see, I think, is that the picture gets us into all kinds of theological trouble as well. Because it is precisely that picture of the ladder and the fall that tricks us into becoming pessimistic in our doctrine of sin. For if we have fallen, then immediately we have to ask, "How far have we fallen? All the way to the bottom? Or perhaps even off the ladder altogether? Have we got any strength left to climb back up?" When we think in terms of the ladder and the fall, these are the questions that naturally follow. Our Roman Catholic friends, who find it quite possible to say that man co-operates with God's grace in "climbing the ladder," can allow that man has some degree of goodness and strength left in him, so that they can avoid the extremist degrees of pessimism. But we Protestants, especially we Lutherans, who hold out for grace *alone,* who insist on the sole sufficiency of God's grace for "salvation," we are virtually forced to become as pessimistic as we can in our doctrine of the fall and sin. If man is to be saved by grace *alone,* we must insist somehow, that there isn't any strength left in him at all, that he has fallen all the way to the bottom—indeed, perhaps off the ladder altogether. So you see what happens: In order to make room for grace, we have to push man down. And then such unsavory things as the doctrine of "total depravity" rears its ugly head. I am reminded of the old story of the Scots Presbyterian minister calling on one of his parishioners who was virtually on her death bed. He was quizzing her about the faith to make sure she had everything right. And he asked her, "Annie, do you believe in the total depravity of man?" "Aye," she said, "'Tis a savin' doctrine!"

So there we are, at the bottom of the ladder, wounded, impotent, and blind! Unable, we tell ourselves, even to begin to climb, totally dependent on some mysterious power we call grace to help us up. It is as though we were just completely drained and tired out and were sitting around waiting for some kind of spiritual vitamin pill or pep pill to get us going again. That, I say, is not a very profound, nor is it a correct view of sin, and it is a blasphemy against God's creative power to boot! It might even be that we like to wallow around in our own weakness so as to excuse ourselves from doing anything—as not so subtle a way of using the doctrine of sin to coddle sin itself!

And the strangest thing is, of course, that this is not what the biblical account of Adam's fall really says. Adam's sin does not consist, we should notice, in *falling down* somewhere. As far as I can gather, the idea of a "fall," in that sense is not biblical at all. Adam's sin consisted rather in succumbing to the temptation to "climb up higher" so to speak, to attempt to invade the province of God. He had been given the sheer gift of life, given the task of caring for the garden, using all his gifts to make it a better place, "subdue" it and cultivate it. But that was not enough. He wanted to be like God. He listened to the voice of the tempter: "Why hang around here and take care of the garden? You can be a God! You were made for better things! You can become immortal!" You can make your own way to the heavens, create your own utopia. The serpent, as the story says, was the most subtle of the beasts of the field. He knew, perhaps, we can say, that if anything God had done too good a job in creation. He had created a man who could be tempted with the highest there is—being a God. He had created a man who could rebel. Sin is not really a falling down. It is rather an attempt to ascend. It is more Promethian, I think, than anything else. It is an attempt to steal from God himself.

This story should warn us about the real subtlety and profundity of sin. It is not that we become something less than man, really, but rather that we have some kind of fateful tendency always to climb up and desert our essential humanity—to leave the garden and go and play at being Gods. What we have lost is not our God-given strength, but rather we have lost faith and broken the bond of creation. Instead of living as though life were a sheer gift, we live as though we had it coming—as though it were ours and we had some kind of rights to it. Luther says somewhere that we ought to live on this earth as though we were living in the guest room of someone else's house. But we don't. We live as though we were the landlords. We tear it up, milk it dry, pollute it, deface it, and step on our fellow men in the process. It never occurs to us that our only real purpose here is to take care of the earth, to take care of our fellow men. We refuse that task and surround ourselves with some kind of myth about ourselves and our destiny. We always have some other goal in mind. We are always on our way somewhere else. Balancing the budget is more important than taking care of people, or "states rights," or whatever. It is not that we have no strength, or that we are so weak, really, but that we are always using it to go somewhere else.

Sin is a disease of the spirit—the pull, the lure of that which is above and beyond, the desire for Utopia, *ou-topos* —"no place." And we should make no mistake about it, sin shows up most subtly precisely in our religious life. It is at the moment that we become religious that the dangers are the greatest. For religion more than anything else can lure us away from our essential tasks. It more than anything else can tempt us to think that we are on our way to some other place on our own steam, that we are really too good for this place. We may pride ourselves on being good and pious, but for all the taking care of the garden we do, it may all be a sham. On the one hand we are really too weak to do anything about it, and on the other we are really on our way somewhere else anyway! *That* is sin.

And maybe in the light of this we can see the significance of the temptation of Christ. For he too was tempted to "climb up higher," to desert the role allotted to him—to use his powers to indulge himself, to tempt God to protect him, to ascend to the throne of the world. But he refused. He stayed here. He stayed with it. He knew there was another way that had to be trodden if men were to be helped. Men must be brought to see somehow where temptation leads. He must bear in his body the wounds administered by men on the make. He had to show us that all our attempts to climb up only drive him to the cross. He had to show us that there is no up, or out, or wherever it is we think we are going. It all leads only to the cross. And he died on that cross at our hands to bring it all to an end, a goal, a *telos*, to teach us to be humans and not Gods, to use our created gifts to take care of this good earth and our fellow human beings. And to see that—really to believe it—is to make his death our death to die to sin in order to live to God. To see that is to be born anew, to receive life back again as a sheer gift.

And that is the meaning of his grace. Grace is not some kind of spiritual vitamin pill for lazy sinners. You are not wounded or impotent or blind in the sense that you have to sit around and wait for some kind of repair job. Grace is simply that power which is strong enough, hopefully, to enable us to stay here, to stay home and "tend to our knittin'," strong enough to get us to begin putting the strength God gave us in creation to the proper task once again. Grace is simply what happens in Jesus Christ, putting an end to the old life, the life of attempting to climb up to heaven or whatever, and giving you back again the life God once gave—the sheer gift. We don't have to beat man down to make room for this grace. Grace is simply the healing of our spiritual disease—our rebellion against being human. In Jesus Christ, in his death and resurrection, we are given once again our essential humanity. Because he died and rose, we need not worry about what is above or beyond, and thus in him sin comes to an end. In him we can turn around and begin to take care of the garden.

My God, My God, Why Have You Forsaken Me?

> *And about three o'clock Jesus cried with a loud voice, "Eli, Eli, lema sabachthani?" that is, "My God, my God, why have you forsaken me?"*
>
> MATTHEW 27:46 NRSV

Today, on Good Friday, we have to listen to these words. They tell us not just of a human tragedy—it is that, of course—but of what the New Testament calls a *skandalon,* a scandal, an offense, an event that shatters all our neat religious view of life, the world, our hopes, desires, aspirations to fit in nicely with God. That he whom we confess to be the Son of God, the pioneer and author of our faith, should cry out to heaven in this fashion staggers the mind and makes us tremble. In the ancient world, a person's dying words were supposed to be an important final statement, a summation, a capstone, so to speak, on a person's entire life. And Jesus cries, "My God, my God, why have you forsaken me?" In Matthew and Mark that is the only word there is from the cross, the last word. After that there is only one last agonizing cry and then the silence of death.

"My God, my God, why have you forsaken me?" Through the years we have had a hard time with these words from the cross, coming from the lips of Jesus. That we should cry out in our suffering in such fashion, though serious enough, is not so strange, for we are sinners. But that *he* should—that shakes the very foundation of our religious world. Can it be true? Was he actually abandoned by God? Is this really a fitting "last word" for him? You see we have a real temptation to turn aside from this word and refuse to hear it. It is too frightening to contemplate. We would prefer a Jesus who did not say words like these, who dies more like a hero; someone whose last words are really encouraging and inspiring. Actually, no doubt, we would prefer a Jesus who doesn't *really* die at all. We would like a Jesus who because he is divine is finally, in his innermost being, protected from death, who dies in calm confidence that it is all going to come out alright in the end anyway. So we have a difficult time allowing these words to sink in, to enter into our religious consciousness. It is too frightening. The prophet Isaiah warned of this long ago:

> For he grew up before him like a young plant,
> and like a root out of dry ground;
> he had no form or comeliness that we should look at him,
> and no beauty that we should desire him.
> He was despised and rejected by men;
> a man of sorrows and acquainted with grief;
> and as *one from whom men hide their faces*
> he was despised and we esteemed him not.

He is as one "from whom men hide their faces." We cannot bear to look, to hear. And the problem is not just that we despised him in life and so rejected and killed him, but then somehow had a change of heart, perhaps, so that now we might all come here together to feel sorry for him; not that we might think better of our terrible mistake and engage in our annual orgy of pity for him. It is not so much, even, I think, that we can somehow draw comfort from the fact that he identifies with us, one with whom we can supposedly empathize. No, the point is that even, and exactly in his death, in these shocking last words, he is one from whom still we hide our faces.

The gospels tell us that when they got him up on the cross, they did not pity him, they mocked him. "He saved others, himself he cannot save. He is the King of Israel, let him come down now from the cross and we will believe in him." Death on a cross was not something to be pitied but only scorned, a death reserved for the most despicable offender, outcasts, and traitors against society. "He looked for some to have pity on him, but there was no man, neither found he any, to comfort him." *Even those crucified with him,* according to Matthew and Mark, mocked and derided him. Even they, apparently, did not feel that Jesus had identified with them. It was, no doubt, the shocking contradiction between his manner of death and what he was supposed to be that called for all the mockery.

All that is bad enough, of course, but now we have to ask whether perhaps the most ironic mockery of Jesus' death may not have been reserved for the time after the resurrection, reserved for his own followers who will not listen to his word from the cross, his own followers who will not accept the reality of his death, his own followers who seek to make him their own religious hero who never really dies, just a convenient moral example perhaps, one who just happens to fit all our needs. We look aside and will not see what is happening. The Son of God is dying, entering into the desperate blackness of death, mocked and derided by everyone and at last forsaken even by God. That is too much. He is as one from whom we hide our faces.

Why? Why is that? Why will we not hear the cry? I suppose it is in the last analysis because we have listened and have our ears attuned to another word, one whispered long, long ago which said, "You shall not die, you shall be like God." Believing that voice, we seem quite naturally to spend most of our lives living as though we weren't going to die, trying to deny, escape, avoid death, the final confrontation that we see on the cross. The rule by which we live is, "Whoever would save his life must take care and not lose it." And that seems logical and indisputable to us. A thinker like Ernest Becker, who wrote a book called *The Denial of Death,* tells us that our whole life project is built on the denial of death. We spend all our energy, all our wit, trying to forget, blocking out, denying that we are mortal, building up a self image, the illusion of character and maturity, trying to make a name for ourselves, refusing to admit that we are just mortal clay, just complicated food for worms. We are always and forever on our way somewhere else, stepping on those who happen to get in our way. So we have a stake in a Savior who doesn't die, a Savior who fits right in with our attempts to build our defenses against death.

But now in the cross we come up against a Jesus, a Savior who goes into the blackness of death with these words, "My God, my God, why have you forsaken me?" as his last word, his final speech. Can this be the last word? What should it mean for us?

It means simply that he dies for us. It means that we can't even manage that, I suppose. He must die *for* us. It means that we must somehow learn to live as beings who are going to die. Indeed, it means according to the New Testament that we have already died. Because he was forsaken, the death we must die has already "been died." But that means that we must hear this word from the cross and let it sound, let it be. Let it be the last word, at least for now. For it is a word which must bring us to our knees, even to our death in him. For if he was forsaken, what chance have we? He himself said it; he reversed the rule by which we live: "Whoever would save his life shall lose it, whoever loses his life for my sake shall find it." There is promise in that. There shall be an Easter, but not without Good Friday, not without his last word. So we must for now let the word sound: "My God, my God, why have you forsaken me?" He alone knows what that means. And we must simply wait for him to whom the question is addressed, wait upon God, for the answer.

> O darkest woe
> Ye tears forth flow!
> Has earth so sad a wonder?
> God the Father's only Son
> Now lies buried yonder.

Father, Forgive Them

Father, forgive them, for they know not what they do.
LUKE 23:34 RSV

Grace to you and peace from God our Father and the Lord Jesus Christ!

"Father forgive them for they know not what they do!" Amid the cacophony of voices in that awful place called "the Skull," one voice continues to sound—through the gloom, the mocking, the scoffing. Jesus is at it again! Declaring forgiveness where it seems useless and hopeless, where he has no right or call to do so. Such behavior, we should recall, is what got him into trouble in the first place. As one prominent interpreter of the New Testament put it, Jesus got into trouble because he forgave really wicked people. Jesus, that is, was not crucified for doing what we would consider evil, for some gross misdeed or sin, he was crucified for what we could only call the good. He was crucified because he forgave sins. And now, from the cross he is still doing it. The cross, that cruel place of execution designed to stop all voices, cannot stop it. The grave cannot stop it. The Father vindicates his cause by raising him from the dead. The forgiveness is to go on.

Still there is something scandalous about this deed, this word from the cross. Jesus forgives people for whom he can make no other plea than that "they know not what they do." A strange thing, is it not? That they should be forgiven because they didn't know what they were doing? And the question that leaps at us from the text is, "Who are these people?" Who are the "they" who don't know what they are doing? Could it, do you suppose, be us? We don't like the idea, I expect. We don't like simply to be lumped together with the "they" who don't know what they are doing. We would rather put ourselves in the role of spectators, those people who, our text tells us, stood by watching. We would more likely put ourselves in the role of those who know the whole story and of course know all about forgiveness and all of that. With the world of today we might well ask, "Who cares about forgiveness?" Are we not more concerned about "self-esteem" and shame and such matters? But now the proclamation from this last word comes back directly: Who cares about forgiveness? Jesus does. He cares enough about it to say it with his dying breath: "Father, forgive them for they know not what they do." Forgiveness is to go on regardless of everything and anything until the end.

So now this word leaves me with but one thing left to do: to speak it again for you to hear so that you may know that it is for you. We are not here to sympathize with Jesus. We are not merely spectators; we are part of the event. If we reckon rightly about what is going on here, we will take our place among the "they" of whom Jesus said, "They know not what they do." For—miracle of miracles—"they" are the forgiven. And so it is that the audacious word can be spoken. In the name of him who this night died that we might live, I say to you, your sins are forgiven. Believe it! It is for you.

Seven Last Words service, Pilgrim Lutheran Church, St. Paul, Minnesota, Good Friday, April 21, 2000

Testimony

The theme for tonight's meditation is testimony. Testimony is a huge word in the Bible, so it is hard to pick one text on which to base our meditation. As a matter of fact the entire Bible is often spoken of as "the testimony." Now I can't preach on the whole Bible. I've got only ten minutes! I have chosen two passages that confront us with a clear picture of the biblical idea of testimony. They are from St. Paul's letters to the congregation at Corinth. I read first from 1 Corinthians 2:1-2, and 2 Corinthians 4:5-6 (RSV).

> When I came to you, brothers and sisters, I did not come proclaiming to you the testimony of God in lofty words or wisdom. For I decided to know nothing among you except Jesus Christ and him crucified. For what we preach is not ourselves, but Jesus Christ as Lord, with ourselves as your servants for Jesus' sake.

Testimony! Not a long word, but large; large because it has a big, important, and powerful family. You all know the family—all those words that begin with "test:" Testament, the Old Testament, the New Testament, last will and testament, testimonial, testify, testate, intestate.

In the Bible, testimony is probably one of the most important words. The two tables of the law were called the Testimony; they were placed in the Ark of the Testimony. The tabernacle was called the Tent of the Testimony. In the New Testament the witness of Jesus Christ, as we can see from the passages of Paul's letters to the Corinthians, is understood as his testimony. Preaching is a form of testimony. In more revivalist churches it was, and still is, a custom for believers to stand up and "give their testimony." We Lutherans have found other ways we think more appropriate for giving public testimony. When we confess the faith and respond in the liturgy or sing hymns, that is our testimony.

Even in our daily lives testimony is an important word. When we are asked to speak the truth, we are called upon to give testimony, to testify to "the truth, the whole truth, and nothing but the truth, so help you God." They are words by which we demand that people be truthful, and so determine what is just or unjust. They are words by which we even try to control the future. We make a "last will and testament" so that our wishes may be carried out even when we are dead and gone.

So we can see, I think, that testimony is a powerful word. It controls much of our lives. It is a word that is supposed to be a vessel for the truth. It calls upon us to give expression to what is in us, in the deepest part of our being. It reveals the truth about us. In the end we will no doubt be called upon to give up our final testimony before the Almighty.

So the question comes home to roost. What shall we say? What is our testimony to the truth? Shall I say that I did my best? Or perhaps that I am a reasonably nice person (most of the time—well maybe some of the time at least); that I think that I have been a good teacher, etc. Is that the truth about me? Or is all that just rather pathetic?

St. Paul in our texts has a quite different idea of what our testimony should be. "For what we preach"—and preaching is really the final and ultimate form of our testimony—"what we preach is not ourselves, but Jesus Christ as Lord, with ourselves your servants for Jesus' sake." Paul, it should be remembered, was writing to the Corinthians. The Corinthians were a lot like us. They had already invented just about every heresy you could imagine. There were, that is, conflicting testimonies. Everyone was impressed with their own status, pursuing their own religious hobby, and bragging about it—I was baptized by Apollos. I by Cephas. I by Reverend So-and-So; he or she is so marvelous and meets my needs. Paul dismisses it all. For what we preach is not ourselves, but Christ as Lord. That is our testimony.

Paul is supremely aware that his own personal life and experience is finally of no particular importance to anyone else but himself. In his letters he constantly plays down such matters. He even refers to them as "refuse" (*skubala*). His life is not the content of his testimony, but Christ. So he insists, "When I came to you, brothers and sisters, I did not come proclaiming to you the testimony of God in lofty words or wisdom. For I decided to know nothing among you except Jesus Christ and him crucified."

Jesus Christ and him crucified! That is the testimony. We have arrived once again at the end of the Lenten season. It is a time for the truth, for once again assessing our testimony. And that means that I too must make my testimony to you. And that can only be finally as St. Paul directs. Jesus Christ was crucified for you; he is Lord; in him your sins are forgiven. That is the testimony.

Forgetting and Remembering

How long, O Lord? Wilt thou forget me for ever?
   How long wilt thou hide thy face from me?
How long must I bear pain in my soul,
   and have sorrow in my heart all the day?
How long shall my enemy be exalted over me?

Consider and answer me, O Lord my God;
   lighten my eyes, lest I sleep the sleep of death;
lest my enemy say, "I have prevailed over him";
   lest my foes rejoice because I am shaken.

But I have trusted in thy steadfast love;
   my heart shall rejoice in thy salvation.
I will sing to the Lord,
   because he has dealt bountifully with me.
PSALM 13 RSV

One of the anxieties we have as human beings is one which arises from the possibility that we may be forgotten. It hurts to be forgotten by one's friends. It hurts deeply to be forgotten by a loved one. It hurts when someone forgets your name, and all of us have experienced that kind of embarrassing moment when someone is wounded by being forgotten. And we wound each other again and again in this way. We have, it seems, just a toehold on existence, just "a foot inside the door" so to speak, and we depend on each other, we live to a large degree to the extent that we are not forgotten by our friends. Being forgotten wounds us, and it cries out for healing.

Sometimes we do magnificent things to escape being forgotten. We may build great pyramids or monuments. Or we may seek, like the heroes of old, to have our name celebrated by the poets and to gain for ourselves a kind of paper immortality. We may write books or plays or poems or music or produce other works of art so that we will not be forgotten. Sometimes we do strange things when we are faced with the threat of being forgotten. We may lash out in anger and rebellion and try to hurt those who have hurt us so that they will at least bear a wound and not forget us—we hope. We do not like to be forgotten because it hurts. Every time we are forgotten, we slip a little from existence.

But all of this, which takes place on a human level, is in a sense, only a parable, a symptom of a much deeper and more fundamental anxiety—the anxiety which arises from the possibility that we may be forgotten by God. Every human forgetting, every leave-taking, every time our name, our face, our deeds are forgotten, the anxiety which this brings is but a prelude which participates in a much greater anxiety, the anxiety that we may be forgotten *forever* —that I will be lost. As Paul Tillich puts it, this is one of the anxieties which make us fear death. It is not the disagreeable and messy business of dying as such that threatens us, but the fear that we may be forgotten eternally. It is this which causes a much deeper and more fundamental anxiety, and cries out for healing. One cannot read the Psalms, I think, without seeing this. Words like those in Psalm 103 are typical:

> As for man, his days are like grass;
> he flourishes like a flower of the field;
> for the wind passes over it, and it is gone,
> and its place knows it no more.

And the psalmist we read in today's lesson knows this anxiety; he cries out:

> How long, O Lord? Wilt thou forget me forever?
> How long wilt thou hide thy face from me?
> How long must I bear pain in my soul,
> and have sorrow in my heart all the day?
> How long shall my enemy be exalted over me?
>
> Consider and answer me, O Lord my God;
> lighten my eyes, lest I sleep the sleep of death;

> lest my enemy say, I have prevailed over him;
> lest my foes rejoice because I am shaken.

This anxiety is something which penetrates to the core of our being, makes us restless in this life, homesick, and often difficult. It is, I suppose, an anxiety which will follow us all the days of this life. There is no easy way out—not even for the Christian. The psalmist, who was a man of God, bears eloquent testimony to that.

But there is a word of healing which sounds among us in spite of our anxiety. The psalmist goes on to declare, "I have trusted in thy steadfast love; my heart shall rejoice in thy salvation." The word of healing is that God remembers. And this is in essence the message of scripture. God remembers. He remembers our plight, he remembers that we are but dust, and—most important—he remembers his covenant. In the beginning of the Gospel of Luke this is one of the great themes which ushers in the story of the Christ. There Zechariah sings, "Blessed be the God of Israel, for he has visited and redeemed his people . . . to perform the mercy promised to our fathers and to *remember* his holy covenant.

In the midst of our anxiety, the anxiety of being forgotten, this word too is heard. It is the essence of the message of Easter and the resurrection. God remembers! It is this word alone which can heal. And perhaps when we listen, and if we listen, then too we can begin to bear the fact that men forget us, and we learn not to expect too much of them—for they are after all only human and we shall all ultimately be forgotten by them. But rejoicing in the fact that God remembers, we can live with them, and understand them, and love them, and say with the psalmist, "I will sing to the Lord because he has dealt bountifully with me."

> Let us pray: Remember us O Lord, when others forget. Speak to us the word of healing and peace. Help us so that we do not expect too much of our fellow humans and to place our trust in thy mercy. In Jesus' name. Amen.

Sermon preached at Luther Seminary chapel

Faith and Doubt

On the evening of that day, the first day of the week, the doors being shut where the disciples were, for fear of the Jews, Jesus came and stood among them and said to them, "Peace be with you." When he had said this, he showed them his hands and his side. Then the disciples were glad when they saw the Lord. Jesus said to them again, "Peace be with you. As the Father has sent me, even so I send you." And when he had said this, he breathed on them, and said to them, "Receive the Holy Spirit. If you forgive the sins of any, they are forgiven; if you retain the sins of any, they are retained."

Now Thomas, one of the twelve, called the Twin, was not with them when Jesus came. So the other disciples told him, "We have seen the Lord." But he said to them, "Unless I see in his hands the print of the nails, and place my finger in the mark of the nails, and place my hand in his side, I will not believe."

Eight days later, his disciples were again in the house, and Thomas was with them. The doors were shut, but Jesus came and stood among them, and said, "Peace be with you." Then he said to Thomas, "Put your finger here, and see my hands; and put out your hand, and place it in my side; do not be faithless, but believing." Thomas answered him, "My Lord and my God!" Jesus said to him, "Have you believed because you have seen me? Blessed are those who have not seen and yet believe."

JOHN 20:19-29 RSV

Our text for today, the Second Sunday of Easter, leads us into the problem of doubt. The central figure in the story, apart from the risen Christ, is Thomas, the disciple who because of his skepticism, his questioning attitude, has come to be known through history as "doubting Thomas." I suppose when we think about it, it seems strange that one of Jesus' disciples, one of the inner circle, one of those whom we like to look up to as being the most faithful, is remembered as a doubter. And yet there is even in this a kind of good news, because it reminds us that these men too were only human and experienced the same difficulties as we, that these men too are companions on our way. For after all, the problem of doubt is always with us. Today especially we are quite conscious of it. Even as Christians we cannot escape the fact that we live in a world where embarrassing questions are asked, that we live in an age of cultivated skepticism, in a time when the old answers, the old systems of meaning don't always seem to suffice, and we are threatened with meaninglessness and doubt. Nothing we can do can alter that fact. We cannot turn back the clock, we cannot run away and hide, much as we may like to. We must learn to live in our age as it is. Christians do not have any special vaccination against doubt.

It is significant, I think, that the New Testament does not seek to gloss over or to steer an evasive course around the problem of doubt—not even in the case of the resurrection. If you read the accounts carefully, you will find that even for the disciples the matter was not as simple as we might think. In Luke's gospel, the 24th chapter, the 11th verse, we are told that when the women told the apostles of the resurrection, "these words seemed to them like idle talk, and they did not believe them." And then even after they had seen Jesus, according to Matthew's gospel, they were not all without their doubts. In Matthew 28:16-17 we read that after the resurrection the eleven went to Galilee where Jesus came to them and that "when they saw him they worshiped him; *but some doubted.*" And then, of course, our text for today about the doubt of Thomas is the classic one in the expression of the doubt that was raised by the story of Jesus' resurrection. The New Testament does not gloss over the problem of doubt, even though it is often glossed over in the church.

When it comes, doubt is something that cannot be avoided. It must be dealt with honestly and forthrightly.

The thing which attracts me personally to the story of Thomas' doubt is the manner in which he states his doubt in such vigorous and almost brutal terms. When the disciples tell him of the resurrection, he says, "Unless I see in his hands the print of the nails, and place my fingers in the mark of the nails, and place my hand in his side, I will not believe." The thing which is striking about the words is their stark, almost coldblooded honesty. Thomas faces his doubt head-on, and he faces the full consequences of his doubt. He will not run away and hide from it. Thomas faces his doubt honestly. The trouble with doubt usually—and the thing which makes it so dangerous and so stifling—is that it tempts us into a life of spiritual dishonesty. Or if doubt comes, we may be led to feel guilty because of our doubts, perhaps even so guilty that we would feel that we are no longer worthy or qualified to be counted among those who are Christians. Doubt then becomes a destroyer, a source of fear and dishonesty.

But it need not nor should it be so. Serious and honest doubt is always an expression of a concern for the truth, and this in itself, certainly, is not a bad thing. That is why it is often said that there is more faith in honest doubt than there is in the belief of many. When belief is just an uncritical acceptance of certain doctrines by virtue of which one thinks he is going to buy off God and achieve salvation, then it is in effect not faith at all, for it is not born out of any concern for the truth. This is what makes the basic honesty and courage of a "doubting Thomas" of more worth than many people's belief. Thomas has a passion for the truth, and he is willing to face his doubt honestly and to deal with it. And this, after all, is the only way doubt can be dealt with. One cannot overcome doubt by refusing to deal with it, refusing to face it. It must be brought out into the open and faced honestly. In the Christian church we ought not to be afraid to speak of doubt. The story of Thomas reminds us of this important fact.

But, of course, our text does not only speak of the act of doubt, it speaks of the conquest of doubt. It does not only tell the story of a doubter, but of the justification of a doubter. For Thomas, this conquest of doubt is brought about by the action of the risen Lord.

He who was wounded appears. He passes through the doors that were closed; he overcomes the obstacles to come to the doubter. He who had stated his doubt in such vigorous terms is now challenged in equally vigorous terms to allay his doubts. Jesus says to Thomas: "Put your finger here, and see my hands; and put out your hand, and place it in my side; do not be faithless, but believing." Thomas can only answer, "My Lord and my God!" The action of the risen Lord, the event of his appearance overcomes the doubt of the disciple. But we ought not to forget that it is to Thomas the doubter that he comes, not to Thomas the believer. Not even Thomas' doubt can separate him ultimately from the Lord. The risen Lord, bearing the wounds of the cross, conquers Thomas' doubt. God justifies even the doubter.

There is something here which we need to remember. We have gotten so used to intellectualizing the faith that we virtually have come to think that we are justified by our right thinking about God. That is to say we seem to think we are justified by virtue of the fact that we don't have any doubts. We are perfectly willing to admit that no one can be perfect morally, that we are all sinners, but we think on the other hand that we must be or that we can be perfect intellectually—by believing all the right doctrines—and that by believing all the right doctrines without any doubts we are justified. We are quick to deny moral works righteousness, but at the same time we seem to think that *intellectual* works righteousness is possible. We forget that God alone justifies not only the sinner, but also the doubter. Paul Tillich, the theologian of our times who had dealt most extensively with the problem of doubt, says that it was this discovery that really enabled him to remain a theologian. In *The Protestant Era* he says:

> The step I myself made in these years was the insight that the principle of justification through faith refers not only to the religious-ethical but also to the religious-intellectual life. Not only he who is in sin but also he who is in doubt is justified through faith. The situation of doubt . . . need not separate us from God. There is faith in every serious doubt, namely, the faith in the truth as such, even if the only truth we can express is our lack of truth. . . . You cannot reach God by the work of right thinking or by

a sacrifice of the intellect or by a submission to strange authorities. . . . You cannot, and are not even asked to try it. Neither works of piety nor works of morality nor works of the intellect establish unity with God. They follow from this unity, but they do not make it.[5]

This is something we need to remember. We are not justified because we don't have any doubts. We are justified by faith—a basic trust in the action of God who comes to us as one who has conquered, as risen Lord, bearing the wounds of the cross. We are justified even as doubters, just as we are justified as sinners.

In this life where our knowledge is always imperfect, there faith and doubt will always be found together, and we shall have to learn to pray as the father of the epileptic in Mark's gospel, "I believe; help my unbelief!" We should not be afraid to admit our doubts any more than we should be afraid to confess our sins. If we are honest, we shall have to admit that we have our ups and downs—even in faith. But when doubt comes, there is always only one remedy—and that is to contemplate him who bore the burden even of our doubt, who was wounded and put to death by it, and yet overcame it. For God does not attempt to overcome our doubt with theoretical arguments; he does not come to us with proofs and systems of thought. He comes to us as one who bears the wounds of our rejection, the wounds of our doubt; he comes to us as one who has born these things and yet conquered—as a risen Lord. He comes as a person who has won this particular victory in this particular event—not as another theory to be doubted.

He comes to us as one who has conquered—who has destroyed all the enemies—gone beyond everything we could do to him. Just as he came to Thomas, he now comes to us in the Spirit, in the Word and the Sacrament; he is acting and will act breaking down the barriers, passing through the doors of doubt to come to us.

Something for Nothing

> *And behold, they brought to him a paralytic, lying on his bed; and when Jesus saw their faith he said to the paralytic, "Take heart, my son; your sins are forgiven." And behold, some of the scribes said to themselves, "This man is blaspheming." But Jesus, knowing their thoughts, said "Why do you think evil in your hearts? For which is easier to say, 'Your sins are forgiven,' or to say, 'Rise and walk'? But that you may know that the Son of man has authority on earth to forgive sins"—he then turned to the paralytic —"Rise, take up your bed and go home." And he rose and went home.*
>
> MATTHEW 9:2-7 RSV

"Take heart, my child, your sins are forgiven." What is supposed to happen when such words are spoken? What is supposed to happen when the gospel is preached, the absolution pronounced? I am going to suggest what I suppose is a rather dangerous answer, so hang on to your seats! Nothing! Nothing is supposed to happen!

Nothing? How, you ask, can you say that? Does there not have to be something? Must it not register and produce results somewhere? But let me ask you a question: What did happen actually when I spoke those words? Perhaps I should try it again: "Take heart, my child, your sins are forgiven!" See! Nothing happened! And perhaps, just perhaps, that's how it should be. For if you think it's dangerous to say that, suppose I were to try it another way. Suppose I were to say, as we are most often wont to say, that when the gospel is preached all sorts of spiritual fireworks were supposed to take place—blinking lights go on in the soul, emotions touch off in the heart and warm feelings in the pit of the stomach, tears in the eyes, and that you are suddenly to become a new person and march off to do battle with wickedness and be different from all the run-of-the-mill ordinary people in the world overnight. That, I suppose, might satisfy our lust for religious triumphalism and propriety, and our programmatic desire for results, but would that be any less dangerous than the first answer?

"Which is easier to say? 'Your sins are forgiven,' or to say, 'Rise and walk'? I expect one of the things that rankled about that word of Jesus is that when it was spoken, nothing really happened. The people could have wondered: How can anyone dare to speak that word here in this place? This place where people sin and are paralyzed and suffer and hurt and kill and die? The word stands in such evident contradiction to the facts. Everyone knows, of course, that *God* in his heaven is forgiving. As Heine says, *C'est son métier,* that is his *business.* But how can one dare to say it here, flat out like that, where everything contradicts it? Blasphemy! Besides, couldn't he think of anything more meaningful to say—as we might put it today? It is hard to imagine that that poor paralytic was exactly eaten up by "guilt feelings." Couldn't he have discoursed with him on the meaning of life or *theodicy* or some such thing?

Of course, Jesus could speak that other word too—if you are curious, if you want a demonstration, if you think that is any more or less of a contradiction to the way things are here. He could say, "Rise, take up your bed and go home." And we are told by our text, simply, that the man rose and went home. I have always been struck by those words—he rose and went home. Is that all? It is almost as though nothing particular had happened, as though he were going out to the barn to do chores, that the normal state of affairs had simply been restored. If it had happened in our day, we can imagine that we would want to run after the man and say, "Wait a minute, Mr. Paralytic, you don't get off so easy!" And reporters could stick a microphone in his face and ask him, "How did it *feel* when the great event took place?" He rose and went home! One would think that at least he would have written a book on religious experience or become a TV evangelist or something! But our gospel writers don't seem to be particularly interested in that sort of thing. It was simply that the truth had been spoken at last—the creative word contradicting the way things are, clearing away all the fog and the nonsense—and that was that.

I often hear it said, "You know, I keep going to church and to chapel, but nothing ever happens!" Well, what do you think should happen? Is God in the entertainment business? Or is it, after all, simply a matter of the truth? And is it not well that we should be reduced to nothing before him, since, to paraphrase one more famous than I, "all our somethings have lighted fools the way to dusty death?" Is it not well, perhaps, that we should taste something of what the mystics of old called the divine nothingness, the "dark night of the soul," through which alone one enters into the truth, the Word which creates *ex nihilo* ?

And so I say it again, because I make bold to claim that I have been sent by him who can also say, "Rise, take up your bed and walk," by him who was raised from the dead and lives forever, sent to say to you, "Take heart, my child, your sins are forgiven!" Maybe nothing happens when I say that. But don't fret, it simply happens to be the truth. And it is just that now God is God, and you are you, and all the nonsense is gone, the slate is clean, and it can begin again. And isn't that something?

Sermon preached at Luther Seminary chapel, Third Quarter, 1975

Endnotes

1 Gerhard O. Forde, *Theology Is for Proclamation* (Minneapolis: Augsburg Fortress, 1990), 1.
2 Regin Prenter, *Spiritus Creator* (Eugene, Oregon: Wipf & Stock Publishers, 2001) 261.
3 Harry J. McSorley, *Luther: Right or Wrong?* (New York: Newman Press, 1969) 307.
4 Ibid., 267.
5 Paul Tillich, *The Protestant Era* (Chicago: The University of Chicago Press) xiv-xv.

www.ingramcontent.com/pod-product-compliance
Lightning Source LLC
Chambersburg PA
CBHW062035120526
44592CB00036B/2142